MY WEEK
AT THE BLUE ANGEL

MY WEEK AT THE BLUE ANGEL

And Other Stories from the Storm Drains, Strip Clubs,
and Trailer Parks of Las Vegas

BY MATTHEW O'BRIEN

PHOTOS BY BILL HUGHES

Huntington Press | Las Vegas, Nevada

HUNTINGTON PRESS
3665 PROCYON STREET, LAS VEGAS, NV 89103
(702) 252-0655, (702) 252-0675 FAX
BOOKS@HUNTINGTONPRESS.COM

**MY WEEK AT THE BLUE ANGEL
AND OTHER STORIES
FROM THE STORM DRAINS,
STRIP CLUBS, AND TRAILER PARKS
OF LAS VEGAS**

PHOTO OF JESSIE FOSTER COURTESY OF GLENDENE GRANT
THE PHOTOS ON THE FOLLOWING PAGES ORIGINALLY APPEARED IN
LAS VEGAS *CITYLIFE*: 7, 13, 41, 45, 106, 122, 125, 127, 131, 155, 163, 167, 197, AND 200.
PHOTOS ON PAGES 139, 142, 157, AND 176 COPYRIGHT BY DANNY MOLLOHAN.
ALL OTHER PHOTOS COPYRIGHT BY BILL HUGHES.

VERSIONS OF THE FOLLOWING STORIES ORIGINALLY APPEARED IN LAS VEGAS *CITYLIFE*: "WHERE'S
JESSIE?" (2/1/07); "HUNTING HUNTER" (2/8/01); "THE LAST TEMPTATION OF LARRY" (9/8/05); "OUT ON
PAROLE" (6/23/05); "DEATH OF THE DOUBLE-WIDE" (10/20/05); "NOTES FROM VEGAS UNDERGROUND"
(6/27/02); "BELLY OF THE BEAST" (8/8/2002); AND "WASTEWATER WORLD" (6/15/06).

To Yolanda Smith and Hunter S. Thompson

ACKNOWLEDGMENTS

The people interviewed in this book

Deke Castleman
and my dad Matt

My mom Liz
my sisters Cathy and Leslie
my brother Eric
my brothers-in-law Peter Gwin
and Tyler Gibbs
my sister-in-law Emily
my nieces Eliza and Julia
and my nephew Timothy

Joshua Ellis
Bill Hughes
Danny Mollohan
and Kat Topaz

Brian Paco Alvarez
H. Lee Barnes
Lindsay Berg
Becky Bosshart
Bill Branon
Su Kim Chung
Johanna Giebelhaus
Joel Gotler
Michael Green
Jarret Keene
Dennis McBride
Chip Mosher
Eric Olsen
Jim Palombo
Brian Rouff
Geoff Schumacher
Cathy Scott
and Chris Staros

and
Laurie Cabot
Anthony Curtis
Heidi Olson
Jessica Roe
and the rest of
the Huntington Press staff

This story collection was born in the storm drains of Vegas.

When my first book, *Beneath the Neon: Life and Death in the Tunnels of Las Vegas*, was published in 2007, several people asked where they could read the two stories that served as background. The stories, co-written by me and Joshua Ellis and published in *CityLife* in 2002, can be found at the alt-weekly's website (www.lasvegascitylife.com), but not easily. The web versions are light on photos and heavy on broken lines. And though the stories are raw, scary, and funny, I wasn't entirely comfortable pointing people toward them.

But, I thought, if I rework the stories, incorporating some of the knowledge gained researching *Beneath the Neon*, they may sit well in a collection.

I thumbed through the archives of *CityLife*, where I'd worked since 2000, searching for other stories to include in the collection. A behind-the-scents tour of the central sewage plant; after 13 years in prison, a convicted murderer tries to adjust to life in Las Vegas; trailer parks closing at a frightening rate, leaving behind broken bonds, promises, and dreams—these stories were good ... and could be improved. (At *CityLife*, I often wished I had one more week to work on a story. I'd soon get that week and more.) They also shared themes: off-the-beaten-path Vegas, beauty in unlikely places, a voice for the voiceless.

In short, they showed a side of the city rarely seen by visitors or locals.

In early 2008, I left *CityLife* to write more independently and creatively. The collection was one of my projects. When not freelancing, I re-researched and rewrote the stories. Then I researched and wrote two originals: "Another Day on Paradise" and "My Week at the Blue Angel." ("My Week at the Blue Angel" blossomed to 19,000 words and became the centerpiece.)

Finally, I updated the stories in an epilogue and photographer Bill Hughes re-shot some of the *CityLife* stories and shot the originals.

The result is *My Week at the Blue Angel: And Other Stories from the Storm Drains, Strip Clubs, and Trailer Parks of Las Vegas.* I hope the collection adds voices to the Vegas dialogue (which is dominated by casino executives, economic analysts, politicians, and tourists), shows a side of "Sin City" you've never seen, and makes you look at the "fabulous" and "world-famous" tourist destination differently.

MATTHEW O'BRIEN | JUNE 24, 2010

WHERE'S JESSIE?

AS THE PLANE TOOK OFF and banked to the south, the United States spread out before Glendene Grant. The Rocky Mountains of Montana. The Snake River and Yellowstone National Park in Idaho and Wyoming. The Great Salt Lake, the Wasatch Range, and Bryce Canyon in Utah.

From her window seat, Grant looked down on the sheet of darkness and thought one thing: Where's Jessie?

Everyone and everything on the flight reminded her of Jessie. The man sitting next to her, who she handed a card with Jessie's photo on it. The TV screen in the seat back, which aired footage of the recovery of two kidnapped boys in Kirkwood, Missouri. Her carry-on bag, containing a laptop, newspaper clippings, and missing-person posters.

The plane began its descent into Las Vegas—the bed of lights, the Monopoly houses, the neon river of the Strip.

Is Jessie somewhere beneath those lights, Grant wondered? Is she alive? Is she dead?

As the plane taxied to the gate, a flight attendant announced a birthday and the passengers sang "Happy Birthday to You." Grant cringed. Jessie was missing on her own birthday. And on Mother's Day. And on Christmas.

So many days in a year. So many reminders.

"They come to Las Vegas to drink and gamble and have fun, and it kind of bothered me that they just assumed everybody else on the plane was there to have fun," said Grant, who lives in Kamloops, British Columbia. "I felt like standing up and saying, 'Excuse me, but I'm not really here to have fun.' I felt like saying, 'After singing 'Happy Birthday,' let's say a prayer for my daughter.'"

Added Jessie's father, Dwight Foster, who flew into Las Vegas from Calgary, Alberta, a few days after Grant, "I saw how spread out the city was and how bright it was and the glitz and the glamour. Of course, the passengers flying in are very excited. Everyone on the plane is going there to have fun and make lots of money. I'm sitting there and all I'm feeling is apprehension and dread and hopelessness. Las Vegas represents a totally different head space for me."

Grant didn't stand up and say anything to the passengers. She doesn't want to be too cynical, she said. She's just sad. Really sad.

She picked up her bag, shuffled off the plane, and made her way through McCarran International Airport.

"I wish I thought that I was coming here to find Jessie," said Grant, her voice breaking. "But I know I'm not going home with her. I know that. Basically, I'm just here to remind people that she's missing and to let more people know she's missing. I just want to bring her picture to light. I just want to try to get some media attention and let the police know we're not giving up. We're not going to quit phoning them. We're not going to quit e-mailing them. We want some answers."

COURTESY OF GLENDENE GRANT

JESSICA EDITH LOUISE FOSTER was born in Calgary on May 27, 1984. She grew up in Kamloops, a city of 90,000 people in south-central British Columbia.

When she was 16, Jessie moved to Calgary to live with her father, who'd separated from her mother when Jessie was one and a half. She graduated from John G. Diefenbaker High School in 2002.

"I missed most of her formative years," said Foster, an occupational health and safety officer with the government of Alberta. "I missed her elementary school years. I missed her junior high school years. So when she moved to Calgary and I was able to sit down with her and help her with her homework, that really helped us bond. We were very close.

"She was a fairly typical young girl," continued Foster, noting that Jessie liked movies, music, and hanging out with friends. "She was a funny and outgoing girl who had her whole life in front of her. I don't know what else to say. I loved her dearly. She was just a really good kid."

In February 2005, Jessie moved back to Kamloops. A few months later, she traveled the United States—Miami, New York City, Atlantic City—with a friend. She ended up in Las Vegas in May of that year and decided to stay.

"I didn't like that she moved here," said Grant, an Internet technician, after checking into the Tropicana. "I even said to her, 'You're not moving to Las Vegas without me having the contact information for somebody else living there.' I literally said to her, 'What if something happens to you? What if you go missing and I don't know who to call?'"

Added Foster, "It was doomed from the beginning. First of all, she was an illegal alien. She was just visiting the United States. Then, shortly after moving here, she met this guy. She was talking about a long-term relationship with him, but she wasn't an American citizen. She wasn't going to be able to live down here with him.

"She didn't think any of this through. How was she expecting this to succeed?"

The guy was North Las Vegas resident Peter Todd, who Jessie moved in with shortly after arriving in Las Vegas.

In November 2005, Jessie flew home to Kamloops to visit. She also visited Calgary. On Christmas Day, the family drove her to the airport and she caught a flight back to Las Vegas.

"If I'd felt I had the right to, I would've stopped her from leaving," said Grant. "But she was twenty-one years old, so I couldn't tell her: 'You have to stay home! You can't go back there!' She was an adult and had been for three years."

It was the last time the family saw Jessie.

On March 28, Jessie's older sister Crystal talked to her on the phone. No one in the family has talked to her since. Her cell phone hasn't been used. Her credit cards haven't been used. She hasn't made any transactions at the bank.

"I knew right away that something was wrong," said Foster. "There was no doubt in my mind. This was not something Jessie had ever done before. She always kept in touch with her family. I broke down, because I knew this was serious."

After several attempts, Grant reached Todd on April 9. He told her Jessie had left him in early April and he hadn't seen or heard from her since. Grant called the North Las Vegas Police Department and the Royal Canadian Mounted Police and reported Jessie missing.

According to a North Las Vegas Police Department report, an officer went to Todd's house that day and asked him about Jessie. Todd told the officer Jessie moved out April 2. He also allowed the officer to look around the home.

A week later, Todd and his ex-wife were questioned at the police department.

"When you're a detective and you interview people, you oftentimes might have a suspicion about this or that," said Tim Bedwell, a public information officer with the North Las Vegas Police Department. "The problem is the law doesn't allow you to use mere suspicion to arrest people, to get a search warrant, and things like that. I'm certainly not prepared to sit here and say there aren't things about this case that are suspicious, but we have to be cautious about what we say. The truth is we don't know what happened to Jessie. We can't even develop any sort of estimation."

In police reports and newspaper stories, Todd has said he had nothing to do with Jessie's disappearance.

In mid-April, Grant and Foster hired private investigator Mike Kirkman of Las Vegas Detectives. Kirkman found out Jessie had been arrested several times for prostitution, under the name Jessie Taylor.

He also discovered that Todd's ex-wife had been arrested for prostitution.

"It shocked me," said Grant. "But then I got over the shock and realized it doesn't really matter what Jessie was doing down here. She was missing and we needed to find her. I don't give a crap what anyone does for a living. They're still human—and I especially wasn't going to judge one of my kids."

Added Foster, "It sounds to me like there's irrefutable evidence that my daughter sold her body for money. I don't care what you call it. I hate the word 'prostitute.' I hate the word 'hooker.' Those things disgust me when I think of them, because that's what my daughter was. That, in itself, is so devastating."

Kirkman also told Grant and Foster he thought their daughter was dead.

Despite shocking revelations and theories, there was little physical evidence in Jessie's disappearance. The North Las Vegas Police Department closed the case pending further information. The Royal Canadian Mounted Police, the Kamloops Police Department, and the Canadian consulate never got involved, said Grant and Foster.

"And that's where the case has been ever since," said Grant. "The only people who have done any further investigation are Mike Kirkman and the family. It's very frustrating."

Said Foster, "The North Las Vegas Police Department doesn't even exist in my mind. They've done absolutely *nothing*. They've done nothing but open a case file. They've disillusioned us and given us great concern about whether any investigation is going to be initiated. They told us right away that they don't have the resources for this kind of case and [Las Vegas] Metro [Police] usually handles these cases and, well, Jessie lived in North Las Vegas. 'Sorry, we have to take the case and we're just not set up for this kind of thing.'

"Basically they said, 'It's our responsibility, but we can't do anything about it.'"

JESSIE'S DISAPPEARANCE HAS AFFECTED her family profoundly. Grant said she's a different person. She doesn't recognize herself. Who have

I become, she sometimes wonders? What have I become?

She was always the loudest, most boisterous person in the room. The one who made everyone laugh. Very outgoing. Now she doesn't even like to leave the house. She's withdrawn. Nothing is fun anymore, she said, now that Jessie's not around.

At one point, Grant was neglecting her three other children. Crystal told her not to forget about them. We need you, too, she said. And you need us.

"It wasn't a matter of not considering them or forgetting about them," said Grant. "It's just that they were *there*. They were in front of me. They were in my house. They were all taken care of and I knew where they were, so all of my energy was focused on Jessie."

It's tough for Foster to describe what a father feels when his daughter disappears without a trace in a foreign city hundreds of miles from home. He can only say he hasn't worked in 10 months. He doesn't do the things he used to do, like camping and swimming. When he tries to do them, he just goes through the motions. There's no passion or purpose. He's numb.

"You go through a period of deep, profound despair," said Foster, "and you live with a lump in your throat and you feel like your chest is going to explode and you feel like your losing grasp on reality. It affected me in ways I never thought possible."

Time passes unnoticed, said Foster. April, May, and June felt like a week. They vanished, along with the good memories—which were replaced by total darkness. Without the e-mails he sent during those months, he wouldn't even have proof that he was alive.

Then time slowed down. To normal. To … a … crawl. August, September, and October felt like an eternity. Time. Stood. Still.

"I get anxious and depressed about some of the most insignificant things," he said, "like driving downtown. I work downtown. I used to just cruise through downtown not even thinking about it. Now I'm looking around at the people pulling up behind me and the people on the sidewalks. Everything's just so surreal."

Jessie's disappearance has gutted him, said Foster. It has ripped him open. He has bled.

Glendene Grant and Dwight Foster

And he will continue to bleed until she's found.

"All along, I hoped the system would work for us. I had faith that once people realized this is serious, this isn't some runaway taking off for a couple weeks, they would do something about it. But they haven't. I was filled with a sense of desperation. I realized that it was coming up on a year since my daughter disappeared—and regardless of all the attempts I'd made to get the local authorities and my consulate to do something, they weren't taking us seriously. It wasn't changing anything. I felt like I had to be a physical presence down here for something to happen.

"Maybe I'm wrong, but I had to give it a shot."

JANUARY 17. ONE FORTY-FIVE P.M. Crime Stoppers of Nevada. Grant and Foster sat in a sterile conference room, their reflections showing on the tabletop. Grant's forearm was wedged between the table and her chin. She was looking down. Foster's arms were folded across his chest. He was looking up. Mike Hope, director of Crime

Stoppers of Nevada, stared at them blankly.

The small talk had ended. The details of Jessie's disappearance had, once again, been reviewed and analyzed. (Grant and Foster added that they thought the "friend" Jessie traveled the United States with was actually a pimp.) The role of Crime Stoppers—to generate tips and try to publicize them—had been defined.

The conversation turned to the $5,000 reward and the possibility of the family increasing it.

"At what stage does a reward start to make a difference?" Foster asked Hope.

"It just depends," said Hope. "We had a homicide a year ago where one hundred thousand dollars brought in a lot of tips. Other times, you get tips for much less than that. There's no magic number. It's just whatever will make someone say, 'That's worth it to me to come forward.' What that number is, I really don't know."

"What do you see as our next move, besides upping the reward?" continued Foster.

"That's about all you can do, as far as Crime Stoppers is concerned. You want to keep the media interested in the story and see if you can entice someone to come forward. There are a couple advertising things I'm going to look into. I can't promise you anything, but I'll talk to some people about billboards and that kind of thing."

I have two daughters myself, Hope said. I know where you're coming from.

"You wake up every single day and you realize another day is starting without her," said Foster. "Where is she? Is she OK? Everything else that seemed important before doesn't even matter. People get so upset about the most trivial things. If nothing else, this has certainly helped put things in perspective."

"Anything that has come up since Jessie's been missing, we just put on hold," added Grant. "We've let a lot of things go by."

Foster leaned forward, placed his elbows on the table, and locked his fingers. His reflection froze.

"If we up the reward to ten thousand dollars, what will Crime Stoppers do?" he asked Hope. "Another press release? TV? Newspapers?"

"What I do is type up the press release. It goes through our public information office. They send it to the newspapers and television stations, but it's up to them whether they broadcast it or not. We don't have any control over that. They may pick it up, they may not. Hopefully it's a slow news day. If there's something big going on, it may get pushed to the bottom of the pile. But we'll certainly do what we can."

"I would really appreciate that," said Foster. "Anything you can do, because it feels like we're spinning our wheels."

Foster told Hope he'd already hit rock bottom. He'd mourned his daughter. In some ways, he'd come to terms with her disappearance. There's only one way for me to go, he said: up. Surprise and happiness if she's found alive. Shock and elation. Love.

Grant told Hope she believes Jessie is alive. That's how I get through the day, she said. That's how I'll get through the rest of my life. That's how I stay strong. I have my whole life to live.

"We may be in different corners on that," said Foster, "but we're together in the search. It doesn't really matter how we feel or what we believe. We just have to find her."

After Crime Stoppers, Grant and Foster visited Las Vegas City Hall. They wanted to bring Jessie's disappearance to the attention of Mayor Oscar Goodman—to appeal to his human side, said Foster. If we're going to find our daughter, he said, we have to get some help from the government. Without it, we're dead.

Let's get some momentum, said Foster entering City Hall. Everybody keeps passing the buck. We want somebody to stand up and take responsibility. We want somebody to say, "You know what? We *do* have a responsibility here! We *do* serve to protect the public! And *this* is what we're going to do for you, Mr. Foster!"

The last time Grant visited City Hall, she was escorted out of the building by security. "Hopefully," she said, "this time there will be a little more respect and they won't treat us like terrorists."

A receptionist and a public information officer took Grant's contact information, but she never heard from the mayor's office.

THE FOLLOWING AFTERNOON, Grant and Foster visited the North Las

Vegas Police Department. They met with Detective Dave Molnar, who was assigned Jessie's case. Molnar, said Grant and Foster, shared some new information with them, but said there were no solid leads. He also told them the police department has to wait seven years to turn a missing-person case into a murder case.

While Grant and Foster met with Molnar, public information officer Tim Bedwell took questions from Canadian TV newscast "Global National" in a conference room.

Is there more the department could do in this case?

"We can't follow leads that aren't there," said Bedwell, a former detective. "We believe we've talked to everyone we know of who has any information in this case, and there's no way for us to develop new leads unless somebody comes forward. There's really nowhere else to follow up."

Grant and Foster said they've given the police department leads it hasn't followed up on.

"Our investigation is about Jessie's disappearance. It's not about what made her decide to come to Las Vegas, although there may be some information in there that's helpful. The reality is this is not an investigation of why Jessie became a prostitute. I know her mother would like to have that question answered, but we're never going to be able to answer it for her. The investigation we're conducting is about what happened to Jessie—and we will follow every lead that has a possibility of helping us determine that."

Does the department have enough staff to investigate this case properly?

"This is not an issue of case workload. This is a matter of not having sufficient leads to follow up on. We can only follow up on what exists. We can't create leads. We can develop leads through other leads. We can develop evidence through investigation. But we can't create people to talk to. The fact of the matter is we have talked to the people who needed to be talked to."

The department has done other things, said Bedwell. Detectives have gone to look at recovered bodies. They fingerprinted a woman in California who matched Jessie's description—blonde hair, hazel eyes, five-foot-six, 125 pounds. They've even followed up on psychic leads.

"I don't want to make us sound desperate," said Bedwell, "because that's not the case. The point is we want to find Jessie as badly as anybody does."

Are there difficulties with the case because she was a prostitute?

"You can't look up the references at her last job interview. You can't talk to the people she worked with, because they aren't going to come forward. People who would've come into contact with her regularly—taxi drivers, male customers, girlfriends—probably worked in the same trade and are not going to come forward. There are a number of barriers to finding people who had contact with Jessie.

"I've worked at three different police departments. I've worked with a number of federal agencies. I have thirty-two years of public service, and I can tell you this department is pursuing this case as far as it possibly can. It's not my goal to convince anyone in the family of that, because they're not going to be satisfied until we bring them their daughter."

Grant and Foster entered the room. Grant's eyes were sunken and glazed over. Foster was flushed. Silence.

Then Foster said there are suspects in the case and the police department needs to go after them.

"Whether you think there's enough evidence to indict someone, under U.S. law there's not," said Bedwell. "We need more."

"Then get more!" said Foster.

"We have enough resources to investigate cases where we *know* a crime occurred—and that's about it. There are a lot of cases out there where we *think* crimes occurred. But if we commit our resources to those cases, we have to pull people off cases where we know crimes were committed. While that's never going to sit well with you, it's a fact."

"I'm not asking you to arrest anyone," said Foster, exhaling. "Start with a block and then put another block on top of it and another and another. It seems to me you have too many rules to operate under and the criminals have all the rights. Goddammit! Where's the case being built? Where's the net being set? How many other girls are going to disappear? How many have disappeared already?"

After the meeting, Grant and Foster drove to Peter Todd's house. A lockbox hung from the doorknob. The windows were dark. Foster started up the walkway, looking down at the concrete.

"I just watched my daughter walk into the house," he said in disbelief. "I could see her. I could see her walking up to the doors. I could see her pulling out her key and walking in and thinking, I'm home. She felt all this was worth what she did for a living. It makes me wonder, did I instill some sort of value in her that made her think *this* is what you live for, do whatever it takes to have a nice home? It makes me wonder if I instilled the right values in her.

"Could I have done something to prevent this?"

ANOTHER SMUT PUBLICATION? Another nightclub promotion? Another huckster trying to sell show tickets?

That's what tourists seemed to be thinking as they approached Grant and Foster, who were handing out missing-person posters in front of the Tropicana. Their eyes averted. Their heads dropped. They veered out of the way.

"Sometimes they don't really notice me until I'm right there," said Grant, clutching a stack of posters. "Sometimes they just have to hear what I'm saying before they'll stop."

Said Foster, "You get everything from absolute ice-cold rudeness to genuine concern. You see the whole range. But this morning, for the first time, I actually had somebody take my arm and physically move me out of the way. He knew what we were doing, too, that we weren't selling anything or trying to give him political dogma. It was the coldest thing I could imagine a human being doing."

During their stay in Las Vegas—Grant was here nine days, Foster five—they gave out 300 posters and 150 cards: "$5,000 Reward. Have You Seen This Woman? We Need to Bring Our Jessie Home!" They walked up and down the sidewalks of the Strip. They stood on the pedestrian bridges. They dropped by the casino security booths.

They hoped to draw people to their websites (www.jessiefoster. ca and www.FindJessieFoster.com) and get them to contribute to their

fund. They also wanted to keep Jessie's face "out there," said Grant.

"Our foster child is a runaway and is missing, too," said Roberta Haight, who lives in the Minneapolis area. "My first reaction to the poster was, oh my God, so many kids in the world are missing and what are we doing to find them? The police don't do anything. That's the sad thing. They just say, 'Well, if they show up, they show up.'"

THE ENGINES GROWLED. The plane jerked. Its nose tilted in the air and its wheels left the runway.

Staring out the window at the kaleidoscope of the Strip, Grant felt hollow. She and Foster had done a lot in Las Vegas—met with Dave Molnar and Tim Bedwell of the North Las Vegas Police Department, visited the house where Jessie lived, passed out hundreds of posters and cards—but she felt she was leaving Jessie behind.

"It's a really big gap not having her here," said Grant. "The hole it leaves is amazing—that one little girl can leave such a big gap in so many people's lives."

At the same time, Grant was glad she was going home. She needed to see her husband, children, and friends. She needed to see familiar faces. She needed to see familiar places. She needed something *sure*.

Grant put her head back and thought about what else she could do for Jessie: a fundraiser at a neighborhood pub, update the websites, more media interviews. Next thing she knew, the plane was beginning its descent into Calgary.

Sitting next to Grant, Foster was numb. He kept thinking about the meeting at the North Las Vegas Police Department. Bedwell didn't understand what I wanted, he thought. He thought I wanted a dragnet. He thought I wanted an arrest. He thought I wanted to trample on the Constitution.

All I want, thought Foster, is a calculated approach. One piece of the puzzle. Then another. And another.

"Glendene and I barely said a word to each other the whole trip home," said Foster. "We looked like two people who had gone through a battle and were sitting back reflecting on it. It's the feeling you get when you've done the best you can and you still don't come away with a win."

But the trip wasn't a total loss, Foster conceded. He got a glimpse into the life of his daughter—maybe the final months of her life. He saw where she lived. He walked in her footsteps. He learned more about what she did for a living. That wasn't how we raised her, he thought. That wasn't how we lived. Who is Jessie Taylor?

"But most of my thoughts were about the vultures and wolves that exist in society," said Foster. "Who don't like the light. Who don't like the attention. And how freely they roam. These days, people look to the skies for terrorists. They think evil is going to drop from the heavens."

But evil walks among us, thought Foster. It's down there beneath all those lights.

HUNTING HUNTER

"THIS IS YOUR NEIGHBOR MR. JONES! Could you please turn the goddamn music down?"

The voice—guttural and cigarette-ravaged—shot from the phone and shook my eardrums. Rolling over in bed, I squinted toward the alarm clock. It read 1:22 a.m.

"I'm not playing any music," I said.

"Just turn the goddamn music down! I'm trying to sleep!"

There was silence as I tried to make sense of the situation. Then the man asked, "Is this O'Brien?"

"Yeah."

"Hunter S. Thompson."

For three weeks, I'd been trying to arrange an interview with the godfather of gonzo journalism. It began with a call to Robert Love, managing editor of *Rolling Stone* (which lists Thompson as chief of the national affairs desk in its masthead). That produced a lead: a phone number for Deborah Fuller, Thompson's secretary.

I called the number immediately. No one answered and the cryptic monotone greeting didn't mention Fuller or Thompson. Unsure I had the right number, I left a message.

Four days passed.

I called the number again and left another message. A few days later, Fuller returned my call and left a message of her own, explaining that she'd been out of town. I called her back—and again got her voicemail.

If his secretary is this hard to reach, I thought, what chance do I have of reaching Thompson?

Finally, Fuller and I spoke and I pitched my story idea: Using *Fear and Loathing in Las Vegas* as a guide, I was going to search for traces of Hunter S. Thompson. Seemingly unimpressed, she told me to fax her the pitch and include my name and number.

A few days later, I called Fuller to see if she got the fax. She said she did, Thompson liked the story idea, and he'd give me a 15- to 20-minute phone interview. Surprised, I told her my deadline. She said he'd call before then—most likely at an unusual hour.

I spent the next week rereading *Fear and Loathing in Las Vegas*, one of my favorite books. I highlighted landmarks: the Mint hotel-casino, the Mint Gun Club, Circus Circus, the Flamingo, McCarran International Airport. I put asterisks by my favorite sections. I wrote notes in the margins: "Interview Debbie Reynolds" and "Is there a room 1150 at the Flamingo?" and "Can this possibly be true?!"

I also wrote questions for Thompson in my notebook: "What do you remember about the Mint?" and "Describe the Mint 400 off-road race" and "What's the most vivid memory of your two trips to Vegas in the spring of '71?" In the morning, I added and scratched off questions. Before going to bed, I put my notebook, tape recorder, and phone tap on my desk.

My deadline passed. I called Fuller, who suggested I send another fax. "Being a journalist himself, Hunter usually responds to deadlines," she said.

Of course, I thought, he's also notorious for *missing* deadlines.

Without expectations, I sent another fax. The phone rang at 1:22 the next morning. I rubbed the sleep from my eyes, stumbled to the desk, and stuck the tap to the receiver. I then pressed "Play" and "Record."

AFTER TALKING TO THOMPSON ABOUT *Fear and Loathing in Las Vegas,* the city, guns, explosives, sex, drugs, and writing, I went back to bed. The alarm clock woke me at eight a.m. I showered and threw on a sweatshirt, cargo pants, and sneakers. Standing over the desk, I stuffed a folder of notes, a map of the city, and an abused copy of *Fear and Loathing* into my workbag. I then packed a lunch and exited the apartment.

The weather was, as Thompson would say, savage. Rain fell at an angle and snow covered the peaks of the northern mountains like aluminum foil. Blue-gray clouds capped the valley. It was 38 degrees.

My search began at Binion's hotel-casino. Formerly the Mint, it's where Raoul Duke and Dr. Gonzo—characters modeled on Thompson and attorney-activist Oscar Zeta Acosta—stayed after driving from L.A. to Vegas in the "Great Red Shark," a Chevy convertible containing "two bags of grass, seventy-five pellets of mescaline, five sheets of high-powered blotter acid, a salt shaker half full of cocaine, and a whole galaxy of multi-colored uppers, downers, screamers, laughers ... and also a quart of tequila, a quart of rum, a case of Budweiser, a pint of raw ether, and two dozen amyls."

I was driving my 1997 Camry. The trunk contained an empty gas can, a basketball, two tennis rackets, a quart of oil, and a case of bottled water. The gas tank, for once, was full. I valet-parked at First Street and Ogden Avenue—like Duke and Gonzo—and entered the casino.

"I remember the Mint vividly," said Thompson, during our 45-minute conversation. "It had a seedy look and feel to it. It was your normal downtown casino, as opposed to the ones on the Strip like Caesars Palace. It was an old-timey place, and there was this big fucking snakelike neon sign flashing outside our window. There were a lot of cowboy hats in the Mint—a lot more than pompadours."

Apparently, only the name had changed at the Mint. The poker room was crawling with leather-faced players in Western wear or leisure suits. Sunburned men in jeans and dusty work boots slumped over the blackjack tables, half asleep. Silver-haired women fed dollar bills to the slot machines, like raw meat to a pack of wolves, while smoking cigarettes and sucking oxygen from wheeled tanks.

It was easy to relate to Duke, who wondered, "Who *are* these people? These faces! Where do they come from? They look like caricatures of used-car dealers from Dallas. But they're *real*. And, sweet Jesus, there are a hell of a *lot* of them—still screaming around these desert-city crap tables at four-thirty on a Sunday morning. Still humping the American Dream, that vision of the Big Winner somehow emerging from the last-minute pre-dawn chaos of a stale Vegas casino."

Like Duke, I bet a dollar on the Big Six's two-dollar spot. The dealer spun the wheel. Click-click-click. It stopped on the dollar spot. You bastards!

Circling the casino, I sat at a slot machine, shook out of the workbag, and removed a crude map from the folder. The map was drawn by K.J. Howe, who worked at the Mint in the early 1970s. According to Howe, I was sitting across from the registration desk, where a stoned, ripped, and twisted Duke and Gonzo were "unable to cope artfully with the registration procedure." I was adjacent to the Zodiac Lounge (now a deli), where they waited for their room and watched lizards gnaw on the necks of guests. And I was 50 feet from the lobby where media registered for the Mint 400, the off-road race *Sports Illustrated* sent Thompson to Vegas to cover.

"I had a list written in red of press people who we had to make sure got credentials," said Howe, who worked the race's registration area in 1971. "One of the names was Hunter Thompson. I remembered that name because it was written in red [indicating the journalist was from a prestigious publication]. I had no clue who he was.

"Well, there was this guy who kept wandering around who obviously wasn't a racing journalist. He just didn't look the part. As I recall, he had on a polyester Hawaiian shirt. To me, that was a dead giveaway that he had nothing to do with the race. In my mind, he was some sort of charlatan trying to get in on the goodies. I figured he was another downtown panhandler or chip hustler.

"Finally, Mel Larson, who was race director at the time, brought him over to me and said, 'You got Hunter Thompson on your list?' You got to be kidding me, I thought! I couldn't believe the guy was a journalist."

Imagining Thompson high-stepping around the lobby—in a fishing hat and aviator glasses, pinching his signature cigarette holder—I put the map back in the workbag and removed *Fear and Loathing*. I flipped to page 28. "This is Doctor Gonzo in eight-fifty" was highlighted yellow. Returning the book to the bag, I searched for the elevator.

On the eighth floor, I discovered there wasn't a room 850; the room numbers ran from 801 to 819. Assuming Thompson made up the room number—he told me *Fear and Loathing* was "a journalism experiment that went awry"—I returned to the lobby and consulted a bellman who has worked at the hotel since the '70s. He said the room numbers weren't changed when Binion's bought the Mint in '88.

Realizing I'd hit a dead end—the photographer Lacerda's room, 1221, also didn't exist—I exited the casino and handed my parking stub to a valet. Waiting for my car, I recalled Duke's departure. He and Gonzo had trashed the room, run up a "fantastic" bill, and didn't pay for a damn thing. Waiting for the Red Shark, holding a satchel stuffed with drugs, weapons, and indecipherable notes, Duke scanned the morning paper and tried to look casual—but he felt guilty about the room and the *Sports Illustrated* assignment, which wasn't taking shape. He set aside the paper and began to pace.

I, too, was apprehensive; my story wasn't taking shape. But I'd picked up the scent of Raoul Duke and Dr. Gonzo—suntan lotion, rum-sweat, and Neutrogena soap—and I was following it wherever it took me.

RAIN RICOCHETED OFF THE WINDSHIELD. The wipers screeched. The smell of sweat, oil, gas, urine, and antifreeze rose from the streets.

Using the same route as the pre-race parade, provided by Howe, I was driving to the site of the 1971 Mint 400. Bonanza Road to Rancho Drive, past warehouses, men in knit caps pushing carts, and day laborers with one hand raised. Rancho to Durango Drive, past taco stands, swap meets, and payday loan stores. I turned right on Durango: horse corrals, scrub desert, virgin subdivisions from the $180s.

"Back that way, around the bend," said a rancher in a truck decorated with dirt. "It'll be on your left."

The road that leads to the Las Vegas Trapshooting Park, formerly the Mint Gun Club, is marked only by a waist-high white sign. I eased onto the road, which was half-gravel and half-asphalt. It rose and dipped and snaked. Around a bend, it rolled through an open gate and into a ravine.

I heard yelling and shotgun blasts.

"Shotguns! No mistaking that flat hollow boom," wrote Thompson in *Fear and Loathing*.

"I stopped the car. What the hell is going on down there? I rolled up all the windows and eased down the gravel road, hunched low on the wheel ... until I saw about a dozen figures pointing shotguns into the air, firing at regular intervals.

"Standing on a slab of concrete out here in the mesquite-desert, this scraggly little oasis in a wasteland north of Vegas, they were clustered, with their shotguns, about fifty yards away from a one-story concrete blockhouse, half-shaded by ten or twelve trees and surrounded by cop-cars, bike-trailers, and motorcycles."

This passage came to life as I coasted down the road. A blockhouse sat straight ahead and a shooting range—walkways, mike stands, traphouses—sprawled to the west. Men in hunting hats and goggles pointed shotguns over the traps, yelled "pull," and fired at clay pigeons. Colored shells surrounded their boots. Bright-orange pigeon fragments were scattered across the range.

I parked in front of a row of trees and entered the blockhouse, which matched the one in the book: single-story, concrete, and containing a bar.

"Officials would hang out in the gun club, running the logistics of the race, all the administrative stuff," said Denny Selleck, who entered a Baja Bug in the 1971 Mint 400. Its rear suspension broke, relegating him to the pits and blockhouse. "But of course, there was plenty of drinking and gambling going on in there. It was like a god-damn zoo. It held a whole mass of people. You were out on the course all day long, from seven a.m. to maybe nine or ten o'clock at night, so it gave you a decent place to piss, get a hamburger, and throw twenty dollars on the pass line."

Shotgun wadding and clay pigeons

I toured the blockhouse, which included a main room, pro shop, and locker room. A gray-haired man wearing glasses stood behind the counter of the pro shop and someone was shuffling around in the locker room. Otherwise, the place was empty and eerily quiet, like a memorial battlefield. Only the tarnished plaques, faded newspaper clippings, and black-and-white photos on the walls hinted at the building's long and colorful history.

Nonetheless, 30 years after the Mint 400, it was easy to imagine the blockhouse bustling with activity: a race official posting results on a tote board; a scar-faced man in a leather jacket pounding the bar and demanding a shot of whiskey; Thompson hunched over a corner table, scribbling notes on a cocktail napkin.

"The racers were ready at dawn," wrote Thompson. "Fine sunrise over the desert. Very tense. But the race didn't start until nine, so we had to kill about three long hours in the casino next to the pits, and that's where the trouble started.

"The bar opened at seven. There was also a 'koffee & donut canteen' in the bunker, but those of us who had been up all night in places like the Circus Circus were in no mood for coffee & donuts. We wanted strong drink. Our tempers were ugly and there were at least two hundred of us, so they opened the bar early. By eight-thirty there were big crowds around the crap tables. The place was full of noise and drunken shouting."

After buying a Jack and Coke at the bar and toasting Thompson, I wandered back outside. A trapshooting tournament had just ended and groundskeepers were raking shells from the walkways, collecting pigeons from the range, and tending to the traps. A man as tall and thin as a Joshua tree, wearing a baseball cap, bluejeans, and work boots, was standing in front of the building. I asked him about the racecourse.

"From what I've heard, it started right over there," he said, aiming his walkie-talkie at a wicket 500 feet northwest of the blockhouse. "That was the start-finish line. I believe the course went north from there, then cut across the desert to the east."

I thanked the man, then walked up the range. Approaching the wicket, I crossed an island of concrete that served as the pits. The northern mountains—Hollywood props when I left my apartment in the morning—rippled like muscles and were unmistakably real. Motorbikes and three-wheelers buzzed in the distance.

"The Mint 400 was an incredible spectacle, but you could barely see it after the first hour because of all the dust the racers kicked up," said Thompson. "After an hour or so, you couldn't see your hand in front of your face. It was like watching the Kentucky Derby in a snowstorm. Everything just disappeared."

Added Shav Glick, who covered the race for the *Los Angeles Times*, "It was a very tough event to cover. There were times you went out on the course, but mainly you just sat in the gun club and interviewed guys as they came in. Then you'd go back to the hotel and write your story. You didn't sit in the stands and watch the Mint 400."

It had stopped raining. The clouds were beginning to break. Standing under the wicket, which was 15 feet tall and 20 feet wide, I watched a three-wheeler bounce across the desert and thought about Thompson. *Sports Illustrated* wanted a 250-word caption on the race; a week late, he filed a 2,500-word frenzy that couldn't be defined—or published. (*Rolling Stone* ran an expanded version of the story on November 11, 1971, and a second part two weeks later. The stories formed the foundation of *Fear and Loathing in Las Vegas*, which was published by Random House in June '72.)

I thought about Acosta. Active in East L.A.'s Chicano community, he was a source for a story Thompson was working on about journalist Ruben Salazar, who was killed by police during a riot. Thompson and Acosta decided to drive to Las Vegas, where they could openly discuss the killing and its aftermath (and Thompson could cover the Mint 400). The road trip was re-created in *Fear and Loathing*, Acosta—who disappeared in 1974 while traveling in Mexico—recast as a 300-pound *Samoan* attorney.

And I thought about the Mint 400: tricked-out motorcycles, dune buggies, and trucks; zero visibility; 400 miles of axle-breaking terrain.

"If you finished the race, regardless of where you placed, you felt awful goddamn good," said Selleck. "If you built a vehicle that'd go 400 miles through that shit—let alone at high speeds—you built yourself one hell of a car.

"The Mint 400 was a son of a bitch. You'd come out of there needing a shower, I promise you that."

LIKE RAOUL DUKE AND DR. GONZO, I cut behind Circus Circus and parked out back. Unlike Duke and Gonzo, I didn't chew mescaline ... or smoke hash ... or sniff ether from a Kleenex before entering the casino.

Fourteen casinos are named in *Fear and Loathing*. Five are still open: the Flamingo, the Sahara, the Tropicana, Caesars Palace, and Circus Circus.

"The city's frightening now; that's my basic reaction to Las Vegas," said Thompson. "It's not the same city I wrote about. It's not the same place at all. You'll notice that even the—what do you call them?—milestone or trademark casinos are gone. I was frightened when I saw the city a few years ago."

Of those five hotel-casinos, Circus Circus seems to have changed the *least* since 1971; something from the book lurks behind every row of slot machines. A safety net stretches over the gambling pit. Acrobats with Eastern European names swing from the rafters and somersault toward the tables. Tightfisted tourists from the Midwest, Middle East, and Asia ignore the acrobats and focus on their cards and chips, which are marked with a creepy clown face.

"The Circus Circus is what the whole hep world would be doing on Saturday night if the Nazis had won the war," wrote Thompson. "This is the Sixth Reich. The ground floor is full of gambling tables, like all the other casinos ... but the place is about four stories high, in the style of a circus tent, and all manner of strange County Fair/Polish Carnival madness is going on up in this space."

I cut through the pit, then climbed a spiral staircase to the Midway—a promenade featuring an assortment of carnival games. Families of eight blocked my path. Balloons burst in my ear. Three-year-olds shrieked for stuffed animals they'll never cuddle with—unless daddy can arc an 11-inch-diameter basketball through a 12-inch hoop ... or throw a whiffle ball into a wicker basket that's set on its side ... or land a quarter on a glass plate from 10 feet away ("No Leaning"). Carnival music filled the air.

Again, I met Thompson's descriptions head-on.

"Meanwhile, on all the upstairs balconies, the customers are be-

ing hustled by every conceivable kind of bizarre shuck. All kinds of funhouse-type booths. Shoot the pasties off the nipples of a ten-foot bulldyke and win a cotton-candy goat. Stand in front of this fantastic machine, my friend, and for just ninety-nine cents your likeness will appear, two hundred feet tall, on a screen above downtown Las Vegas. Ninety-nine cents more for a voice message. 'Say whatever you want, fella. They'll hear you, don't worry about that. Remember you'll be two hundred feet tall.'"

Circling the Midway, I found refuge in the Horse-A-Round Bar. The Merry-Go-Round Bar in *Fear and Loathing*, it's where Gonzo got "the Fear" and refused to leave until the carousel-bar stopped spinning. Ten people—mostly parents in need of a drink—were scattered about the place, which is bordered by tables, booths, and plastic horses. It wasn't spinning.

"It hasn't been working all day," said the bartender, setting my Jack and Coke on a cocktail napkin. "I don't know what's wrong with it."

As I sipped my drink and flipped through *Fear and Loathing*, another circus act was introduced. A clown balanced plungers on its chin. A long-haired man with a Russian name, whom I assumed was a struggling actor from L.A., performed a gymnastics routine. The acrobats took to the air.

Thompson described a similar act in the book.

"Right above the gambling tables the Forty Flying Carazito Brothers are doing a high-wire trapeze act, along with four muzzled wolverines and the Six Nymphet Sisters from San Diego ... so you're down on the main floor playing blackjack, and the stakes are getting high when suddenly you chance to look up, and there, right smack above your head is a half-naked fourteen-year-old girl being chased through the air by a snarling wolverine, which is suddenly locked in a death battle with two silver-painted Polacks who come swinging down from opposite balconies and meet in mid-air on the wolverine's neck ... both Polacks seize the animal as they fall straight down towards the crap tables—but they bounce off the net; they separate and spring back up towards the roof in three different directions, and just as they're about to fall again they are grabbed out of the air by three Korean Kittens and trapezed off to one of the balconies."

Said Ralph Steadman, who illustrated *Fear and Loathing*, "When I finally visited Circus Circus in 1975, I understood what Hunter was visualizing. It was very strange. All the acrobats flying above the net and so forth. It was surreal. When I saw those people sitting around the gaming tables, I thought of Nazi Germany and the Weimar Republic. I used all these rather inhuman characterizations to express these people, who were bored, hardened, and bitter. I felt that had to be expressed."

While visiting Vegas in '71, Thompson hung out at Circus Circus; a few of his musician friends had a steady gig at the casino's Gilded Cage lounge.

But his experiences at Circus Circus were more mundane than Duke's.

"Circus Circus was a strange scene," said Thompson, "but in retrospect, it doesn't seem essentially weird. By the time I got around to going to Circus Circus, I had been surrounded by strangeness for so long that I kind of took it for granted. It didn't seem all that unusual at that point, particularly since I was there to see some friends who were playing in the lounge. Of course, I did try to buy an ape in that place."

Thompson said an old man who was part of an act at Circus Circus owned an ape. He walked it around on a leash, said Thompson, and even let it hang out at the Horse-A-Round Bar.

"Well, I kind of took a liking to the ape," said Thompson. "It had a good sense of humor and was like a precocious kid. I offered the old man eight hundred dollars for it. I remember it clearly. It seemed like a good idea at the time."

Mike Hartzell, a ringmaster at Circus Circus in the 1970s and now director of entertainment, said Thompson probably tried to buy "Boobie," an orangutan owned by Jon Berosini. Berosini and his son, Bobby, had an ape show at the casino in the early '70s.

Hartzell knew little about Thompson's experiences at Circus Circus, but shared one of his favorite stories about Boobie.

"After the show, the Berosinis used to put the apes on a cart and roll them down a ramp past a snack bar on the main floor," said Hartzell. "They'd usually let Boobie walk beside them, because he was so friendly.

"One time Boobie went by a guest who was sitting at the snack bar eating chicken and took a leg off the guy's plate. He then began chewing on it and walking away. Well, the guy got up, whirled Boobie around, punched him in the nose, and took back the chicken leg. He then said some rude things to Boobie and his owner and started gnawing on the leg."

Sitting in the Horse-A-Round Bar, head buzzing and book opened, I wondered if that guest was Thompson. Nah, I decided. That's not his style. He would've shot the ape with a .357 magnum or blown it to bits with a stick of dynamite.

Maybe the guest was Acosta, I thought. Yeah, that seemed to make more sense. Judging by everything I'd heard and read, he was a crazy son of a bitch—and perfectly capable of punching an orangutan in the nose, taking back a chicken leg, and gnawing on it defiantly. I could actually *see* Acosta, as played by Benicio del Toro in the movie *Fear and Loathing in Las Vegas*, doing it. Stirring my drink, I cracked a smile.

Sensing the circus act was coming to a close, I tried to beat the crowd to the casino. I paid my tab, put the book in the bag, and climbed off the stool. Circling the Midway, I angled for the staircase. The promenade was cluttered with strollers, pregnant women, and red-eyed runny-nosed kids dragging stuffed animals by the ears. (Even when dad does the impossible, the little buggers aren't happy!) Swerving to the left, I squeezed past the Chicken in a Pot booth—where the objective is to catapult a fake fowl into a pot by hitting a spring with a hammer—and found the stairs.

THE SUN MELTED THE CLOUDS LIKE COTTON CANDY. As I turned right on the Strip and started south, a beam of light broke through and bounced off the taxis and fountains and hotel-casinos. I popped the glove compartment and put on my shades, then rolled down the windows. Above the crane-cluttered skyline, the clouds scattered like a pack of rats in the beam of a flashlight.

The lanes of Las Vegas Boulevard, usually stop-and-go, were loose. Passing the Desert Inn, I recalled the scene in *Fear and Loathing* in which Duke jumped a series of curbs and parked on the sidewalk in front of the casino. Fashion Show mall flashed by the passenger-side window; on this section of the Strip, once home to the Silver Slipper, Duke and Gonzo drag-raced two "hoggish-looking" couples in a blue Ford with Oklahoma plates. The Venetian … the Mirage … Caesars Palace. Cabbies spoke with their horns. Exhaust fumes fouled the air.

I made an illegal U-turn, then disappeared into a driveway between Barbary Coast and the Flamingo.

Leo Lewis, general manager of the Flamingo from 1974 to 1978, met me at the casino's main cage. Five-foot-three and 125 pounds, wearing a light-blue cardigan sweater, turquoise jeans, and cowboy boots, Lewis had agreed to help me search for traces of Thompson—who checked out of the Mint, returned home to Woody Creek, Colorado, then checked into the Flamingo a month later to cover the National District Attorneys Association's Conference on Narcotics and Dangerous Drugs.

"The Flamingo had a different crowd than the Mint," said Thompson. "The Mint was strenuously promoting itself as an A-list place, but it never really got there. It was still much seedier than the casinos on the Strip. However, the Flamingo appeared to be a top-of-the-line hotel. But any place that hosts cop conventions—well, you never know."

I asked Thompson, who's 63 years old, if he had any vivid memories of his trips to Vegas in '71. "Jesus Christ, yes!" he said. He clearly remembers driving to the Mint Gun Club, he said, and checking into the Flamingo.

"The lobby was crawling with cops," said Thompson. "I mean, they weren't advertising themselves as cops. They weren't waving their billy clubs in the air. But once you took a second look at them, you could tell they were all vicious rubes from hick towns across America."

In *Fear and Loathing*, Duke tiptoed out of the Mint and—drunk and paranoid—drove halfway to L.A. He then drove back to Vegas, traded in the Red Shark for the White Whale (a convertible Cadillac Coupe deVille), and checked into the Flamingo.

"The place was full of cops," wrote Thompson. "I saw this at a glance. Most of them were just standing around trying to look casual, all dressed exactly alike in their cut-rate Vegas casuals: plaid bermuda shorts, Arnie Palmer golf shirts, and hairless white legs tapering down to rubberized 'beach sandals.' It was a terrifying scene to walk into—a super stakeout of some kind. If I hadn't known about the conference my mind might have snapped. You got the impression that somebody was going to be gunned down in a blazing crossfire at any moment—maybe the entire Manson Family."

Duke and Gonzo rendezvoused in mini-suite 1150. They then proceeded to infiltrate the drug conference (held catty-corner to the Flamingo at the Dunes), trash the suite, and terrorize the maids.

I hoped Lewis, whom I reached through the Flamingo's PR department, could help me find the lobby where Thompson checked in and the general vicinity of his suite. It didn't seem like too much to ask; Lewis, I assumed, had been in the lobby hundreds of times and the book described the suite in detail. (It had a big gray door and was in a far wing of the hotel, overlooking the pool.)

But Lewis looked lost and paged Director of Cage Operations Brenda Stewart, who has worked at the Flamingo since 1973.

A few minutes later, Stewart arrived at the cage. She and Lewis took a stroll down Memory Lane, then I explained the mission: find the lobby and the suite. Lewis and Stewart—who had high hair and an east Tennessee drawl—debated the layout of the old Flamingo, neither sounding confident. Finally, Lewis and I followed Stewart through the casino and outside. She started up a sidewalk that bordered the Strip, into a stream of tourists. Lewis lagged behind. I was halfway between them, serving as a beacon.

Past a gantlet of men handing out adult-entertainment fliers, Stewart stopped at a side street. She looked down the street and pointed out a few reconfigured features of the Flamingo, none of which were the lobby or suites.

Returning to the casino in search of another longtime employee, Stewart slipped between two blackjack tables and into a pit. Lewis leaned against one of the tables, breathing heavily.

"You OK, Mr. Lewis?" I asked him.

"I'll be all right," he said. "I had a triple bypass about a year ago. Boy, was it a killer! But with this damn Alzheimer's, I don't remember all that much about it."

Alzheimer's! I almost dropped my notebook and pen. I make 15 calls to track down the former general manager of the Flamingo, arrange to meet him in the casino, and he has *Alzheimer's*? You bastards!

On cue, Stewart slipped out of the pit and said the employee she was looking for was off today. I sagged. Lewis shrugged. Undeterred, Stewart started up an aisle created by the tables and weaved through a maze of slot machines. She stopped in front of a wall lined with black-and-white photos: Benjamin "Bugsy" Siegel, Dean Martin and Jerry Lewis, the Flamingo in the late 1940s. Using exterior shots of the hotel from the '50s, '60s, and '70s, we tried to figure out where the old lobby and suites would be located today.

We were interrupted by a cocktail waitress. An employee of the Flamingo since 1967, she recognized Lewis and stopped to say hello. When told we were looking for the old lobby and suites, she smacked her gum and pointed toward Bugsy's Bagel Company.

"The lobby was right over there," she said, "and the suites were in the back by the pool."

Giving up on the lobby—which apparently had been built over—Lewis, Stewart, and I set out for the suites. Again, Lewis lagged behind and was breathing heavily. I reviewed the steps of CPR: tilt head back, pinch nose, four quick breaths. (Or is it three breaths?)

After stumbling down some stairs, we exited the hotel and entered a courtyard cluttered with rocks, palm trees, and man-made ponds. Lewis seemed to gain his bearings. Leaning over the railing of a bridge, between tourists posing for pictures, he stood on his toes and pointed toward the eastern horizon.

"The suites were over there!" he said. "I remember when they tore them down! Actually, I tore them down when I ran the place!"

"Not much for history, huh?" I said, standing behind him.

"Well what in the hell was I going to do with them?"

I thought about giving him a smart-ass answer, but didn't. Old-school Vegas casino execs aren't usually amused by smart-ass remarks and I was too tired and frustrated to think of one. All I could do was laugh ... and wander deeper into the courtyard.

Approaching the pool, I thought about the suite. It, according to *Fear and Loathing*, contained evidence of "excessive consumption of almost every type of drug known to civilized man since 1544 A.D." It was also where Gonzo seduced Lucy, a runaway from Montana who was obsessed with Barbra Streisand.

A source familiar with the book and movie told me that Thompson—not Acosta—seduced a young woman in Vegas. That was changed in the book, the source said, because Thompson was married at the time.

When I asked Thompson if this was true, he hesitated.

"Jesus, what kind of fool were you talking to?" he said. "There are scenes in the book that had to be toned down—but no, I found her in the room. What are you trying to do, say my crimes were attributed to Oscar?"

"No," I said. "I was just looking for an anecdote."

"If you're looking for an anecdote, here's one that comes to mind."

Thompson told me that when he boarded a plane to fly to the Conference on Narcotics and Dangerous Drugs, he noticed the district attorney of Aspen, Colorado, was on the flight. He knew the DA, so he said hello. During a layover in Denver, Thompson discovered the DA was also en route to the drug conference. Worried he'd blow his cover, Thompson told him he was infiltrating the conference and made him promise to keep it a secret. Laughing, the DA agreed.

"So all along," said Thompson, "the DA of Aspen knew exactly what I was doing."

A plaque pulled me from my thoughts. In front of the wedding chapel, it said the suites were located in this area of the courtyard from December 26, 1946, to December 14, 1993. There were 77 rooms, including Siegel's—which featured bulletproof windows and five exits (e.g., a ladder leading from the hallway closet to an underground garage).

But Bugsy's preoccupation with safety proved to be misplaced, the plaque said. On June 20, 1947, at the Beverly Hills home of his girlfriend Virginia Hill, he was shot several times through a window and killed.

Realizing my hopes of finding the suite were as dead as Siegel, I reunited with Lewis and Stewart. I thanked them for their time, then cut through the courtyard—visions of Lucy's Streisand portraits dancing in my head—and angled toward the parking deck.

DRIVING SOUTH ON THE STRIP—Bellagio, Paris Las Vegas, the new Aladdin—I considered turning on Tropicana Avenue, merging onto I-15, and searching for the North Star Coffee Lounge. It was tempting; *Fear and Loathing* provided plenty of clues about the lounge's location and the scene stands out in the book.

After drag-racing the Okies, Duke and Gonzo pulled into the parking lot of the North Star—an all-night diner on Tonopah Highway in North Las Vegas. It was three a.m. The place was empty. A woman with muscular arms, a square jaw, and a balloon chest stood behind the counter.

"The waitress had the appearance of a very old hooker who had finally found her place in life," wrote Thompson. "She was definitely *in charge* here, and she eyed us with obvious disapproval as we settled onto our stools."

Duke ordered coffee and a hamburger. Gonzo ordered a glass of ice water—with ice. He drank it in one gulp, then asked for another. The waitress sneered.

A few minutes later, Gonzo scribbled "Back Door Beauty?" on a napkin and handed it to the waitress. She balled the napkin, threw it at him, and called him a "spic pimp."

He pulled out a knife. She froze.

The only thing cut was a phone cord, but the scene was charged with tension.

"There have been a lot of scripts based on *Fear and Loathing* written in the past twenty or so years and not one of them included the North Star scene," said Terry Gilliam, who directed *Fear and Loathing in Las Vegas*. "When I was going over the book again, before we started working on our script, that scene jumped out at me because it was so different from everything else. It's ugly. It's unforgivable. It really sticks out because most of the other scenes in the book have a bit of madness to them, but you never feel people are being victimized.

"The North Star scene crosses the line. It goes too far."

Added Marco Acosta, Oscar Zeta Acosta's son: "I remember dozens of incidents where my dad and Hunter were playing around with guns and dynamite, shooting at each other and blowing things up. They did a lot of crazy stuff like that, so I have no doubt the scene actually happened. My dad always carried a weapon, usually a knife or a gun—and he wasn't afraid to pull it out."

The scene may have happened, but not at a North Star Coffee Lounge on Tonopah Highway. According to city directories, longtime residents, and police officers who worked the beat in the early 1970s, there was no North Star Coffee Lounge. In fact, there were only a few all-night diners in the area—none of which fit the description.

I wasn't in the mood for another wild-goose chase, and the Spring Mountains were swallowing the sun, so I crossed Tropicana and continued south on the Strip—the same route Duke took when driving Gonzo to McCarran airport and missing a turn. Excalibur ... Luxor ... Mandalay Bay. The airport sprawled to the east. Stopped at a light, I removed the book from the bag and flipped to page 170.

"We were flashing along at good speed," wrote Thompson. "I was looking for an opening, some kind of access road, some lane across the runway to the terminal. We were five miles past the last stoplight and there wasn't enough time to turn around and go back to it."

The light turned green. I hit the gas, steering with my right hand and holding the book open in my left.

"I hit the brakes and eased the Whale down into the grassy moat between the two freeway lanes. The ditch was too deep for a head-on run, so I took it at an angle. The Whale almost rolled, but I kept the wheels churning and we careened up the opposite bank and into the oncoming lane. Fortunately, it was empty. We came out of the moat with the nose of the car up in the air like a hydroplane ... then bounced on the freeway and kept right on going into the cactus field on the other side. I recall running over a fence of some kind and dragging it a few hundred yards, but by the time we got to the runway we were fully under control ... screaming along at about 60 miles an hour in low gear, and it looked like a wide-open run all the way to the terminal."

Looking over his shoulder for approaching planes, Duke accelerated. Gonzo—wide-eyed and ashen—hung onto the dashboard with both hands. Runway ... cactus ... runway. Three minutes and 15 seconds till takeoff.

Spotting the red-and-silver Western airliner, Duke pulled up behind a van and Gonzo jumped out. Duke pointed the Whale toward a break in the fence ... and floored it. In the rearview mirror, he saw Gonzo board the plane. He then exited the airport through the break and disappeared into traffic on Paradise Road.

Could this scene *possibly* be true, I wondered? Did Thompson miss the turn to the airport, run over a fence, and drive to the terminal? Is he *that* fucking crazy?

"Actually, there was an opening in the fence," said Thompson. "There was no time. Oscar was going to miss his plane. I'd taken a wrong turn somewhere and we could see the plane, but we couldn't get to it until I saw an opening in the fence. I went through it and drove him right up to the terminal."

I was skeptical, but McCarran employees and locals familiar with the airport said this was possible in the early '70s.

"I don't know if Thompson did it or not, but it could certainly be done," said Bob Leavitt, a self-described "ramp rat" who hung out at the airport in the '70s. "Back then, before airport security got to be such a big deal, there was no fence north of the old Bonanza hanger. On the Strip side, if you wanted to check out the airport, all you had to do was drive out there. Thompson could've driven right into the airport and—if he was crazy enough—gone right across the runway."

As I passed the "Welcome to Fabulous Las Vegas" sign—"Drive Carefully Come Back Soon"—a Southwest Airlines 737 tilted its nose to the sky and roared. I looked at the plane, then at a fence surrounding the airport; it didn't have any breaks, and plastic bags were tangled in the barbwire. I decided to take the long way to Paradise Road.

Picking up Duke's trail, I turned right on Russell Road and left on Maryland Parkway. I passed UNLV, then took a left on Flamingo Road. The sun had fallen behind the Spring Mountains, silhouetting the flat peaks and the hotel-casinos on the Strip. The mountains looked like waves that were breaking on Bellagio, Caesars Palace, and Paris Las Vegas and flooding the valley. Driving into the sunset, I thought about one of my favorite sections of *Fear and Loathing*—the end of Chapter Eight, which eulogizes the drug culture of the 1960s.

"There was madness in any direction, at any hour," wrote Thompson. "If not across the Bay, then up the Golden Gate or down 101 to Los Altos or La Honda. ... You could strike sparks anywhere. There was a fantastic universal sense that whatever we were doing was *right*, that we were winning. ...

"And that, I think, was the handle—that sense of inevitable victory over the forces of Old and Evil. Not in any mean or military sense; we didn't need that. Our energy would simply *prevail*. There was no point in fighting—on our side or theirs. We had all the momentum; we were riding the crest of a high and beautiful wave. ...

"So now, less than five years later, you can go up on a steep hill in Las Vegas and look west, and with the right kind of eyes you can almost *see* the high-water mark—that place where the wave finally broke and rolled back."

THE LAST TEMPTATION OF LARRY

I'M NOT A REGULAR AT LARRY'S VILLA. And if I were, I wouldn't admit it.

One night three years ago, I ended up at the strip club with my friends Josh and Saab. Josh provided a running commentary on the music, which ranged from classic country to commercial hip-hop. I remember him laughing at the dancers and customers who were singing along to Springsteen's "Born in the U.S.A.," seemingly oblivious to the fact that the song is a critique of America.

"Born down in a dead man's town/The first kick I took was when I hit the ground/You end up like a dog that's been beat too much/Till you spend half your life just covering up."

Meanwhile, Saab was putting his artistic skills to use. Low on cash (as usual), he tipped the dancers with portraits penciled in his reporter's notebook. This went over well—initially. The women pulled the piece of paper from their G-strings, unfolded it, and discovered not a crude comment or phone number, but a big-eyed soft-lipped rendering of themselves. They giggled like schoolgirls.

But Saab's act soon grew old. After five minutes of flirting and grinding, the dancers pursued a different kind of paper—one that actually helped pay the bills.

"I got to go back to work, baby," I overheard one young lady tell Saab, as she slid out of the booth and disappeared into the darkness.

A few years later, on a Friday night, my friend Adam and I were trying to figure out what to do. One of us brought up the Villa.

"I've never been there before," said Adam.

"What?" I was flabbergasted. "It's like Paris, man. Everybody has to go there at least once."

Wading through the main room, Adam and I sat in a corner booth and surveyed the scene. The room was bright—too bright—illuminating scrawny tattooed strippers and leather-clad customers. The stage was empty, the go-go poles tarnished.

Adam wasn't impressed—or amused. As the strippers and cock-tail waitresses ignored us, his mood soured. We don't mind being ignored at Club Paradise or even Play It Again, Sam—but this was too much. We left a few minutes later.

As I recall, that's my experience with Larry's Villa. However, I've always been fascinated with the club. I've wondered about its dancers, its customers, and—most of all—its owner. Who's Larry? What's his story? How many gold chains are draped from his neck?

A month ago, I called the club in hopes of answering these questions. I explained I was a reporter interested in talking to Larry. To my surprise, he returned my call the next day.

"Hey, Matt," he said. "It's Larry LaPenta. Boy, have I got a story for you!"

"What's going on, Larry?"

"Here's the headline: 'Strip club owner finds religion!'"

I laughed. "What do you mean?"

"I'm starting my own church!"

WALKING INTO LARRY'S VILLA AT NOON is a strange experience—much stranger than walking in at midnight. I felt like I was entering a cave. As the door closed behind me, the backlight faded. Darkness crashed down on me. My eyes adjusted. I closed and opened them to speed up the process, but it didn't help. I couldn't see anything for at least five seconds.

It was eerily quiet—no Aerosmith, Nine Inch Nails, or 50 Cent. Finally, the stage came into focus. It was empty, as were the booths.

I made out two silhouettes stooped over the bar. One pinched a cigarette with its left hand and punched the buttons of a video poker machine with its right. The other, a man who was hunched over, turned around and climbed off the stool.

"Are you Matt?" the man asked.

"Yeah."

"I'm Larry."

I did a double take. I don't know what I expected Larry to look like, but this wasn't it: gray hair, red face, floppy ears. He was dressed in a plaid short-sleeve shirt, leisure pants, and loafers. His Mayor Oscar Goodman nose supported square-framed glasses. Suspenders pulled the waistline of his pants up high—belly-button high. He looked like a Summerlin retiree.

After explaining that the girls don't go on until one p.m., Larry escorted me to a neighboring office. He sat behind an island-sized desk. I sat in front of it.

As I suspected, the 83-year-old LaPenta had lived one hell of a life. He grew up in Connecticut during the Great Depression. His mother died when he was eight, he said, his father when he was 15. He never finished middle school.

When he was 20, Larry joined the Navy. He served in Europe during World War II and was later stationed in San Diego. In 1945, the year before Benjamin "Bugsy" Siegel opened the Flamingo, Larry came through Las Vegas on a troop train.

"Boy, was I impressed," he said, adding that he'd spent much of the war years in cold climates. "Downtown was only two blocks long, but it was something else. I remembered how much I liked it and I came back."

LaPenta moved to Las Vegas in the late 1940s, when its population was less than 50,000. He worked as a waiter for several years, he said, serving Howard Hughes, the Rat Pack, and members of the Mob. When he dropped an authentic "fuggetaboutit," I shifted my feet.

"Were you ever affiliated?" I asked him. "You know, connected with the Mob?"

"No," he answered. "But you couldn't be a maitre d' in Las Vegas at that time and not rub shoulders with the Mob. Hell, they'd come to you to open the doors and to be waited on. I witnessed a whole lot of transactions. You kept your mouth shut, your head down, and you just did your job."

While working as a waiter, Larry launched a business career. He opened a hot-dog stand, a lunch counter, and a restaurant. In 1972, he opened a piano bar called Larry's Villa at the corner of Rancho Drive and Bonanza Road.

The bar was nice, said LaPenta, but it didn't make much money.

"One day, a customer said, 'Larry, for crying out loud. Why don't you get some broads in here and let's have some fun?' At that time, the topless thing was happening in New York, Miami, and all the big cities. I said, 'You're crazy. I wouldn't know where to start.'"

The customer suggested Larry put an ad seeking dancers in the newspaper. He did. To his surprise, it got a response.

"That's how it started," said Larry, leaning forward and resting his elbows on the desk. "We took a piece of plywood that had one good side and we set it on top of two cocktail tables in the corner. We had three wooden steps from a trailer house or something, and we'd hold the girl's hand to get her up on this rickety thing. Within a month, you couldn't get in the place."

Since then, Larry's Villa—the first strip club in Las Vegas—has expanded three times. And while not as big as Sapphire or as popular as Olympic Garden, it does pretty well.

"We're always busy," said manager Ron Lenox. "Quite often, we're busier than a lot of the bigger clubs in town."

When asked how much money the Villa brings in, Larry balked. He didn't want to talk numbers. But noting that he owns land and other businesses in Las Vegas, he said he's worth about $15 million.

So what does he want to do with all that money? How does he plan to give something back to the community? What's his last wish?

To start a church, of course.

"I came up with the idea when I read Thomas Paine's *The Age of Reason*," said LaPenta, who carries the book with him everywhere

Larry LaPenta

he goes. "I don't even remember how or when I came across it, but it really impressed me. Here's the thing that intrigued me the most: All religions are based on mythology, make-believe characters; Thomas Paine actually lived. We have his picture. We have his writings. There's no bullshit involved here, no lies.

"Did Jesus write anything?" he continued, veins popping from his neck. "Moses? Mohammed?"

I was stunned by Larry's intensity. He spoke with a passion that was, frankly, kind of creepy. I wondered if he was serious. Or crazy.

"So wait," I said, checking my tape recorder to make sure it was working. "Money you've made from Larry's Villa is going toward starting a church?"

"Absolutely. Just because I own a topless bar doesn't mean I'm not religious. I have scruples and morals."

I tried to recall *The Age of Reason* from my high-school civics class. What was its message? What did Paine advocate? Bible-burning? Church-burning? The extermination of all Christians?

But like most high-school students, I didn't pay any attention to the book.

"What kind of church will it be?" I asked Larry.

"We'll believe in God and all good things," he said. "We'll believe that God is good and certainly not evil. We'll have prayer. We'll believe in being patriotic Americans. In a way, I hope to start an all-American church. It will focus on self-improvement and current events, not the past. We'll look for good causes to get involved in."

"Who do you think will attend this church?"

"All the people who are not heavily into religion. All of the agnostics and nonbelievers."

"A church for atheists?"

"Skeptics."

"You'll practice a sort of nonreligious religion?"

"We'll believe in the good things about religion, but none of the dramatics and rituals. We don't want all that."

I paused to take a breath. Larry had given me a lot to think about—none of which was really registering. "You're serious about this?"

"Very serious," said Larry. "It's something I really believe in. I believe religion has gone crazy, has gone astray. It's bad for the world—and I want to do something to help make things better."

AUTO SHOPS, PAYDAY LOAN STORES, and fast-food restaurants flashed by the car windows. Then the Las Vegas Valley Water District, Skinny Dugan's Pub, and Carpeteria. I was headed west on Charleston Boulevard, looking for the 4300 block. Finally, I turned into a strip mall at the corner of Charleston and Arville and parked.

Climbing out of the car, I scanned the mall, which was all brick and aluminum. A gay club sat at the west end, a kung-fu school at the east end. A mattress outlet, candle shop, and black-windowed loan store were wedged in between. I glanced at my notebook to make sure I had the right address.

I approached the space at 4351 West Charleston hesitantly. Mirrored tint covered the door and windows, and "Tuxedo Rentals Special $49.99" was burned across the facade. I pulled on the door. It was locked, but a man in a paint-spattered cap and overalls cracked it open.

The main room was rectangular, white, and as sterile as a doctor's office. A wooden pulpit and an American flag stood on a stage in one corner and a framed copy of the Declaration of Independence and a portrait of Thomas Paine hung from a wall. (Obviously, I had the right address.) Otherwise, the room was empty. It looked like an election campaign headquarters that had long ago been abandoned.

Dressed in a black suit, a red, white, and blue tie, and shiny loafers—clutching *The Age of Reason* like the Bible—Larry entered the space through the back door. He shook my hand, then gave me a tour. Leaning into a half-painted nook, he said it would serve as a café for members of the church. The pail-cluttered cubicle in the corner would be an office, he said. Shuffling out of the front door and looking up at the facade, into the harsh Mojave glare, he declared, "It's going to say, 'Thomas Paine's Church of God and Common Sense.' The sign's on the way."

Larry and I (Don Quixote and Sancho Panza?) walked back into the main room. He stepped onto the stage and stood behind the pulpit, looking like a Southern Baptist preacher. I asked him if he'd given the church any more thought.

"It's going to be a church for patriotic Americans," he said. "It'll be nondenominational, nonsectarian. Basically, we want us all to be better Americans, to unite, and to do what we can to improve our lives and our country."

After complaining about illegal immigration and complimenting Fox News commentator Bill O'Reilly, Larry said he started a mailing list to let people know about the church, he plans to run ads, and some of his employees have expressed interest in attending the first meeting.

Leaning against the pulpit, still clutching *The Age of Reason*, he said he signed a two-year lease and plans to use the space daily. Activities will include self-improvement meetings, a Toastmaster's (or public-speaking) night, and current-events debates.

"I'm going to give it two years," he said. "If it makes it, great. If it doesn't, that's OK, too."

If the church does well, Larry would like to expand. He hopes to eventually open branches in Boulder City, North Las Vegas, and throughout the state and country.

"If this develops, I'd like to make it my work," he said. "I'd like to make it my main project. I've lost interest in making money. What's the point? We could all drop dead at any moment.

"I've done a lot in my life. I've been on boat cruises. I've traveled around the United States in my motor home. I've traveled through Europe. I've been there and done that. Now I want to do something that feels good, that feels rewarding. If it doesn't work, at least I can say I tried. But I think it has potential because of all the patriotism going around today.

"Who knows? I've got everything to gain and nothing to lose."

IT WAS SATURDAY NIGHT ... and beggars, laborers, and prostitutes lined the curbs of Bonanza Road near Rancho Drive. The smell of chicken grease from Popeye's polluted the air. The roar of U.S. Highway 95 drowned out everything. I tapped the brakes, turned into Larry's Villa, and weaved through the parking lot, which was cluttered with pickups, delivery trucks, and Harleys.

I parked, then approached the Villa—a squat, windowless build-

ing made of cinder blocks and Spanish tile. A sign on the front door read, "Please No Motorcycles on the Sidewalk." A reasonable request, I thought as I entered the club.

A short woman with a bob was on stage, twirling around the pole in stilettos that could kill a vampire. She dropped her dress straps, revealing her fake breasts. Crumpled dollar bills littered the catwalk.

Through the fog, I made out Larry at a table on the far side of the club. We'd agreed to meet, a week and a half after touring the church, for a final interview. I wanted to find out what progress (if any) he'd made and if he was having second thoughts. I also wanted to see the Villa in its full blue-collar glory.

I swung around the bar, which was lined with men in tank tops and jeans, and joined Larry at the table.

"We've been here for more than thirty years," he said, looking around the room proudly. "I was very fortunate that I had a long-term lease and that the landlord has been really good to me. We're the ones who started the strip-club craze in Las Vegas. I never realized it would grow into such a big thing."

AC/DC's "You Shook Me All Night Long" faded out. Cueing up another track, the DJ cut on the mike with a crackle. "Hey, guys, that was Kaitlyn doing it for you. Give her a hand. Monroe is making her way onto the stage. Pay attention."

I asked Larry about the dancers at the Villa—April, Bella, Trina, Sidney, Serenity, and all the others.

"They're nice people," he said. "They couldn't work here if they weren't. They can't do drugs. They can't drink too much. It's not allowed. We'd have to fire them. We're running a legitimate business here."

Metro Police records support Larry's claim. The club has only been cited once, in 1995 for hiring an employee who didn't have a work card.

"We have some of the better dancers in town," added Lenox. "Most of them know the tricks on the pole. A lot of the other clubs don't do the pole work. We have some of the most beautiful girls around."

On cue, Dallas—bleach-blonde hair and librarian glasses—slithered from the shadows and said hello to Larry. I asked her if she'd heard about the church and was going to attend the first meeting.

"I'll probably check it out," said Dallas, who's danced at the club for three and a half years. "I've been going to church since I was a little girl. Just because I'm a stripper doesn't mean I'm not religious or I don't have beliefs."

As Dallas scaled the stage, two men in mud-stained T-shirts, jeans, and work boots approached the bar. Their baseball caps turned backward, they ordered Buds. I looked around the room. Huddled in the booths, sucking on Marlboros, bearded men stared up at the stage.

"What about the customers?" I asked Larry.

"Naturally, we have a working-class crowd, but it's steady and consistent. Some of these people have been coming here from day one."

Dan Prior, a truck driver based in Southern California, swears by the Villa. When he's in Las Vegas on deliveries, he always drops in.

"If Larry's Villa were to close, I wouldn't know what to do," said Prior. "It would devastate me. My friends are here. I know all the bartenders on all three shifts. That's what Larry's is to me. It's one place I can go to see all my friends."

Asked about the church, Prior shook his head and smiled.

"When it comes to Larry, he's going to do what he wants to do. I don't see anything wrong with him starting a church. Yeah, it is funny in a sense. Here's a man who has owned a strip club for more than thirty years; for him to turn around and start a church kind of contradicts itself. But whatever Larry wants to do, he should do. I'm all for it."

I asked Larry if he'd made any progress with the church. He smiled and said the sign—a red, white, and blue behemoth—is up, the interior of the space has been remodeled, and chairs have been set up in the main room.

The first meeting is next Sunday, he said.

"It sounds strange for a strip-club owner to talk like this, but America's in trouble," said Larry, as 50 Cent's "In da Club" faded in and the women began to writhe. "We need American citizens to support our country and to be good patriotic Americans. That's what I want to promote.

"I'm going for it. It's what I'm going to do the rest of my life, and I'm going to give it the best shot I can."

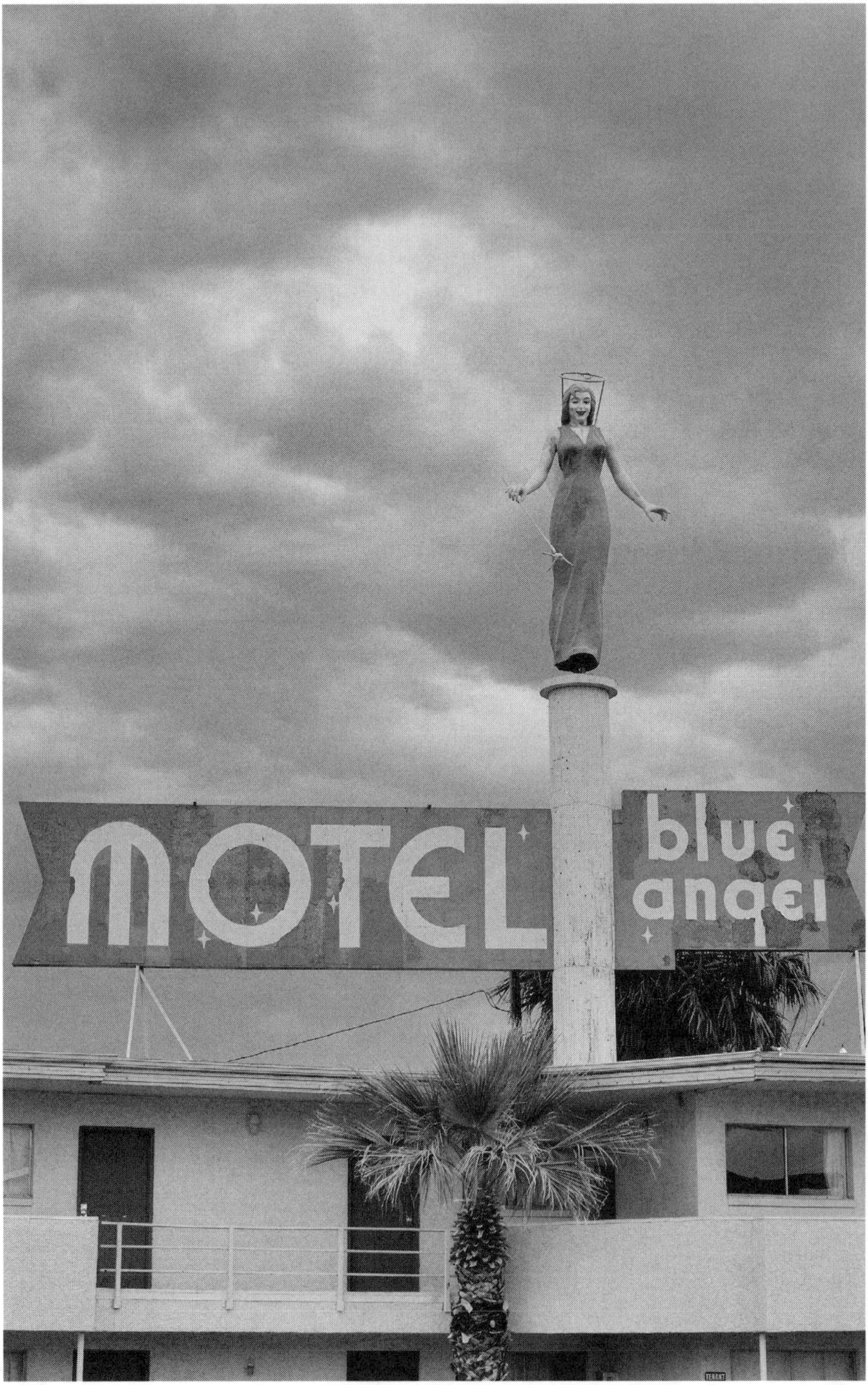
MOTEL
blue
angel

MY WEEK AT THE BLUE ANGEL

THE BLUE ANGEL MOTEL SITS at the bottom of Fremont Street in a neon graveyard where the signs still advertise "Color TV," the swimming pools are filled with gravel, and the rent money is earned at the blood bank. No valets or bellmen or doormen here. Just madmen (and madwomen). It's a two-story motel … with a million stories.

Rooms at the Blue Angel are $130 a week—there are no daily rates—cash only. The motel provides towels, toilet paper, and tension. Nothing else. BYOS (bring your own soap).

The rooms include four blank walls (or maybe an abstract painting hung upside down), a ceiling, bed, dorm fridge, sink, toilet, and shower. Need to make a call? Use the pay phone on Charleston Boulevard. During your stay, you'll be inspired—but there's no pad and pen on top of the nightstand. You'll talk to God—but there's no Bible in the drawer.

If the walls were to fall—and soon they will—you'd see tattooed couples fighting and fucking, widows in wheelchairs watching "Judge Judy," Vietnam vets fastening on their limbs. You'd see 250-pound women reading romance novels in bed, slick-haired men leaning on walkers and clutching beers, runaways scrawling poetry into their diaries.

Tenants (no one even pretends to call them guests) include strippers, prostitutes, panhandlers, handicappers, day laborers, landscapers, construction workers, fast-food employees, convenience-store clerks, and every other make and model of lost soul and hustler imaginable (and unimaginable).

The motel's driveway, which connects Fremont and Charleston and serves as a shortcut, has kissed more shoes than tires. It's a death march led by thirst, hunger, and addiction. The ultimate walk of shame. Grocery carts rattling in the 100-degree night, as Mack, a full-blooded German shepherd, snarls atop the office.

And a 10-foot-tall angel looks down on it all, waving her wand and, magically, still smiling after all these years.

MONDAY

I threw my bags into the back seat of the cab, climbed in, and said, "The Blue Angel Motel."

The driver was updating his logbook. He capped the pen, snapped the book shut, and adjusted the rearview mirror. "Oh, OK," he said, looking at me in the mirror. "On Fremont Street, right?"

"Yeah," I said. The two-way radio crackled. A talk-show host ranted on the AM dial. Heading north on Paradise Road, I assumed the cabby was wondering why I was going to the Blue Angel. Sex? Drugs? Suicide? "I'm going to spend a week there, just to get away from my apartment. I'm a writer. It looks like an interesting place."

"You going to do research or what?"

"I guess you could call it that. Just check in and check out the place and see if it inspires me. Maybe research some of its history. There are tons of weekly motels in Vegas and I've always been curious about what they were like in their prime, who used to stay there, and who stays there now. What do you know about the place?"

"I don't know anything about it. I suppose it does have history. The only thing is, if you want to get history, you got to talk to people who've been here awhile, not the transient population. You'd be better off going to a senior center. If you want to know what happened years ago, talk to seniors. They know everything."

"I thought cabbies knew everything. That's why I'm taking a cab down there."

"Well, I'm telling you where to go. Go to the sources. And the sources are now living in senior centers. People that have been here thirty or forty years, they have so many stories. The women that have been kept women. The guys who know where the bodies are buried in the desert—the ones who broke hands and kneecaps with baseball bats. Guys who came from Chicago, Kansas City, New York, Detroit.

"Seriously, you'd forget about whatever you're going to write and change your direction."

I looked out the window. The sun was setting and law offices, massage parlors, and low-rent apartments blurred by. My mind drifted. Cabbies are paid to route passengers to strip clubs. Are they also paid to route them to senior centers? What's this guy's deal?

I noticed we were approaching Las Vegas Boulevard.

"You going to take a right at the Boulevard and go down to Fremont?" I said.

He didn't respond.

"Everybody fits into a certain survival mode," he said, making the turn, "and they usually can't get out of it. That's how they survive. They fit into their little niche, and that's about it." He paused. "Yeah, very few people are free birds. Even the ones that say they're free, they're not. They just have a different type of armor on."

The dispatcher sent a cab to Tony Roma's on Sahara Avenue. The talk-show host trashed Al Gore, calling him a "con man" who's "made a fortune peddling fear and apocalyptic prophecies." Wedding chapels, tattoo parlors, and pawnshops blurred by.

"I've traveled all over the world," continued the cabby, "and I've found that people are the same everywhere you go. Basically, they want to live their lives uninfluenced by government and society and religion, but those three entities usually screw up everything for people. They can't live a happy life. They can't do what they want to do without harming other people. A lot of times they're forced into choices they don't really want to make, actions they don't really want to take."

He turned on Fremont. Hipster bars, used-car lots, weekly motels.

"The only thing you have to do is face your fears," he said, looking at me in the mirror. "They really won't hurt you that much. I mean, they're painful, but they're less painful than you think they are. That's all I can say."

I looked at him in the mirror. He had Coke-bottle glasses and bloodshot eyes. A balding head, graying beard, and bulky shoulder peeked out from behind the driver seat.

"Is there something you picked up on?" I asked.

"I pick up on everything that everybody does. My calling would've been to go into a ministry; I probably would've ended up a cardinal or something like that. But instead, I'm driving a cab."

From a forest of signs, the word "Motel" and five sparkles came into focus on the south side of the street. Then two Carolina-blue arches. And finally, an angel on a pedestal hovering over a cluster of white stucco buildings.

"Here we go," I said. "If you could just drop me off at the office."

He turned into the driveway.

"Remember what I told you," he said. "Don't think that your little fears are big ones."

He parked in front of the office. I squinted at the meter, which read $16.70, then handed him $25. He counted it and gave me back five dollars.

"No," I said. "That's for you."

"I don't need it. My wife's a retired police officer, so we do pretty well."

"Oh, come on."

I tried to give him the five dollars, but he wouldn't take it. So I grabbed my bags, opened the back door, and climbed out. As I approached the office, which was white brick and one story, my mind was racing. Why didn't he take the money? Was it something I said? Something I did?

Whatever the reason, it seemed like a bad omen. I felt like Ishmael boarding the *Pequod*. I thought about jumping ship—catching a cab home and checking in another day—but I kept walking toward the office. The door ("No Soliciting") opened with a squeal, the bell rang for service, and the blurred image of a red-haired woman in an orange dress appeared behind a Plexiglas window.

"Yeah," I said. "I want to get a room."

"All right."

"Do you have daily rates?"

"No. Just weekly."

"OK."

"All right. That'll be a hundred and fifty dollars; a hundred and thirty for the room and a twenty-dollar deposit. And I need to see an ID."

I reached for my wallet and placed my driver's license in the tray beneath the window. "Do you have anything that looks out onto the parking lot and Fremont?"

"Let me see," she said, disappearing into the shadows.

I looked around the office, noticing a watercolor painting hanging on the far wall. Titled "French Kisses," it featured a tree in the foreground, a country house in the background, and a man and woman hugging and kissing in the middle ground. I wondered how many people had re-created that pose at the Blue Angel over the years.

The woman reappeared. "A room right across the parking lot is available. The maids just got finished with it. They said the pipe under the sink may be leaking, but you can take a look at it if you want. Everything else is ready to go."

"I'll take it."

"OK. Just read and sign the motel rules and registration slip."

As she placed two pieces of paper in the tray, I noticed a tattoo on her upper left arm. It appeared to be a name surrounded by hearts and roses.

"What's the tattoo on your arm?" I asked, picking up the pieces of paper.

"Oh, it's just a man's name. My ex-husband."

"And those are hearts and roses?"

She didn't respond.

I read the rules (management is not responsible for personal property or injury, no pets allowed, the maximum stay is 28 days, etc.), then signed them and the registration slip with a pen chained to the counter.

"Do you take debit or credit?"

"No. Cash only."

I put $160 in the tray. She replaced it with a $10 bill, a copy of the registration slip, and the key to room 124, which I slipped onto my chain.

Entering the room, I was greeted by the smell of smoke—not fresh smoke, but smoke that seemed to date back decades. It wasn't just in the carpet, bedsheets, and upholstery of the room, I sensed, but in the walls, ceiling, and vents. The roaches and bedbugs smell like smoke, I imagined as I opened the curtain.

A full-sized bed covered with a polyester blanket shimmered in the middle of the room. I dropped my bags, walked to the bed, and pulled back the blanket, which was riddled with cigarette burns. The sheets were scratchy, but clean. No bugs or suspicious stains.

I dropped to my hands and knees, feeling the stiff carpet, and looked under the bed. No underwear, weapons, or bodies.

The adjoining room, which had a ceramic-tile floor, consisted of a closet, mirror, and sink. The cabinet doors of the sink were open, exposing the pipe and water damage to the board beneath it. But now, the pipe and board were dry.

The toilet and shower were in a separate room, stark and cramped. A half-roll of toilet paper stood atop a steel holder and a "Sanitized for Your Protection" seal was wrapped around the seat. Staring at the seal—the only touch of class in the room—I cracked a smile.

Returning to the main room, I approached the window. A circular wooden table topped with a gym towel, roll of toilet paper, and place mat emerged from the shadows. The towel was marked *BAM* in black ink and the mat featured an idyllic seaside scene: gulls silhouetted by a half-sun, couples frolicking in the sand, tilting sailboats.

I looked out the window. A "Beware of Dog" sign hung from the chain-link fence surrounding the pool, which was filled with gravel. In an area of the parking lot cordoned off with caution tape, tenants stood around a smoking grill, talking and eating. Ah yes, I remembered. Memorial Day. For a year of service in the jungles of Nam, you get free hot dogs at the Blue Angel Motel. A buffet at the El Cortez casino (when you present a valid military ID). A spin on an oversized slot machine at the Western. Thanks for your service, soldier! See you next year ... if you're still around!

I turned away from the window, threw my bags on the bed, and began to unpack. From my duffel bag, I removed four shirts and two pair of pants and hung them in the closet. A pair of Chucks found the closet floor, a floppy hat the top shelf. I set my shaving bag and a bottle of mouthwash next to the sink, then flung the duffel bag, brimming with underwear and socks, into the closet.

From my workbag, I unsheathed my laptop and set it on the place mat. A notebook and tape recorder joined the strange still life:

towel, toilet paper, mat, laptop. *Literary Nevada: Writings from the Silver State* landed on one of the nightstands, a cell-phone charger on the other. Finally, I stacked six DVDs, including *Der Blaue Engel* (*The Blue Angel*), on the dresser, between a 17-inch Zenith and the dorm fridge.

After transcribing the notes from the cab ride and check-in, and watching the end of Game Four of the NBA Western Conference Finals (the Nuggets beat the Lakers 120-101), I walked to Pepe's Tacos and ate dinner. I returned to the room at 11 p.m. and fastened the chain lock, which was hanging by one loose screw. I turned the button lock on the doorknob. Then I reached for the sliding-bolt lock ... and realized the bolt was missing. Fishing into my pocket, I removed a ballpoint pen and threaded it through the eye.

I washed my face, brushed my teeth, and killed a cockroach with the DVD case of *Very Bad Things*. Then I killed the lights and cracked the curtain. The silhouette of a man pushing a grocery cart crept across the parking lot. Above the wheezing air conditioner (actually a light switch-activated chiller), I could hear the cart rattling and Mack (the guard dog owned by the motel's maintenance man, who lives above the office) snarling. I looked up at the angel. She was twisting in the wind, her back turned toward me.

TUESDAY

A white Mercedes-Benz weaved around the island of palm trees and pool and parked in the breezeway ("No Trespassing") that bordered my room. A few minutes later, a gray-haired man in glasses climbed out of the car. He was wearing a salmon-colored button-down shirt and brown slacks and loafers. I shook his hand, then escorted him to the room.

From a window of the Blue Angel, it probably looked like a drug deal or strange sexual liaison—but it wasn't. The man was Bob Stoldal, a longtime Las Vegan, newsman, and historian. I invited him to the Blue Angel, which opened in 1958, so I could get a better sense of the motel, Fremont Street, and the area.

"Holy cow!" he said, entering the room. "That smoke's pretty potent."

"Yeah, you get used to it after a while, but it knocks you on your ass when you first come in."

"No artwork on the walls."

"No. It's pretty bare. But I guess if you're on the streets or between homes and you're looking for a place to crash, this wouldn't be that bad."

"Yeah, you can sit at the table. You got the bed, dresser, closet. And this is a nice little piece of architecture."

He ran his hand over the room's one unique design feature: three pieces of wood, each seven feet long and five inches wide, standing on the border of the main room and bathroom, angled like opened blinds.

"Yeah, it is," I said. "But I can't figure out what it's for."

"It gives you more of a sense of openness, rather than just walling it off. You get a feel of expanse." He tapped his foot on the tile floor. "This is new."

"Yeah, looks polished."

Bob and I worked our way back to the main room. I closed the curtain, hid the laptop under the table, and opened the door.

"You ever been to the Blue Angel?" I said, as we exited the room.

"No. Now I officially have."

Locking the door, I looked over my shoulder. "You've never spent the night here?"

"No."

"Oh, come on, Bob. I won't tell anyone."

He smiled. "No. But in high school, this driveway was a shortcut between Fremont and Charleston. We'd flash through here in our cars. It was just part of being a teenager in Las Vegas in the nineteen fifties and sixties."

As we approached the pool, pigeons flew from the chain-link fence and landed on the roof of the motel. We leaned against the fence. Two dog bowls sat inside the gate and weeds grew from the gravel.

"Do you remember when the pool had water in it?" I said.

"Sure," said Bob, who moved to Las Vegas in 1957 and graduated from Las Vegas High in '58. "It was a nice pool, but we didn't think about it much in those days. Most of the time we were here, it was six or seven o'clock, after we'd gotten our homework done and were cruising around."

"What do you think when you see the pool now?"

"My first reaction is it's a sad, sad sight. Why don't they just bulldoze it and pave it over, rather than leave this monument to yesterday? Are they saving it so when this area returns to prominence, they can just take the gravel out? I don't think so. Bulldoze it and give yourself more space and not have this constant reminder that this is a failing business and failing area."

"I wonder why, exactly, they filled the pool in. How does it benefit them?"

"I think there are multiple reasons, but the primary reason is money. It's really about the cost of upkeep and insurance. And if the pools in this area brought customers in, they'd still be fully operational, but they're no longer drawing the clientele. The motels are drawing a different clientele that's not staying in Vegas for one or two days and lying out by the pool. They're folks who are using the motel as their home."

We pushed off the fence and continued across the parking lot, toward Fremont. In the middle of the lot, we stopped and looked at the angel. She had yellow hair, red lips, and white skin and was wearing a light-blue evening gown that bunched at her feet. In her right hand, she pinched a five-pointed wand that waved over the motel.

"I tried to take a picture of her a hundred times," said Bob, "before I finally realized she moves."

"It's strange. Yesterday, all I could see from this angle was her back. She was facing east. Now we're seeing her profile. She's facing north."

"But she's not moving. I wonder if the wind pushes her wings."

"Yeah, I think so."

"When I was down here a couple months ago, I was taking pictures of her and I had to drive all the way around in a circle. She was doing a three-sixty, but it looked like she was powered by a motor. It doesn't look like it now, does it?"

"No," I said, studying her profile: sharp nose, double-D breasts, heart-shaped wings. "What do you know about the sculpture?"

"Betty Willis, who designed the 'Welcome to Fabulous Las Vegas' sign, designed it. It's been the subject of a number of photo shoots, postcards, and documentaries. It's been used to symbolize the decay of downtown Las Vegas. As you pan down from the angel, which seems to be in pretty good shape, you can see that the sign itself is in disrepair."

The sign, ribbon-shaped and parted by the pedestal, read, "Motel Blue Angel." It was faded, its paint chipping. Pigeons nested in its cabinet.

Bob turned toward Fremont and continued across the lot. "You know," he said, "this used to be Route Sixty-Six."

"I didn't know Route Sixty-Six cut through Nevada."

"Actually, this was Four-Sixty-Six. When Hoover Dam was built, the state of Nevada got permission to take an alternate route of Sixty-Six at Kingman, Arizona, that would come up Fremont, make a left at Las Vegas Boulevard, and pick up Sixty-Six at Baker, California. It was that way from nineteen thirty-five to sixty-one, and it was listed as part of Route Sixty-Six. Businesses along this stretch would use that to their advantage. Many of the motels would advertise that they were on Boulder Highway or Highway Ninety-Three or Route Sixty-Six, anything that would give them some status."

Reaching the sidewalk, I turned around and looked at the Blue Angel.

"Is it typical of the motels that were built along this stretch in the fifties?" I said.

"It's one of the younger motels," said Bob, who's researched local motels for more than 10 years. "It broke ground in fifty-seven, when most of the motels along east Fremont were single-story. It was a big place. It didn't have a convention facility, per se, but it had that idea. There were meeting rooms. West of the motel was a full-scale restaurant and next to the restaurant was the Blue Onion drive-in. This complex was buzzing with activity. If you squint, in some ways it hasn't changed all that much. The angel's still there. The building's pretty much the same, with the light-blue doors. The palm trees. The only thing that's changed is the pool and the clientele."

"How's the clientele changed?"

"Well, in the late fifties, upscale motel guests stayed at the Blue Angel. It was the newest motel on east Fremont and it had all the state-of-the-art things, so it attracted folks that wanted that kind of experience. Now you got the other end of the economic scale. It offers weekly rentals and it attracts folks that can't afford apartments for a full month. They'll check in for a week or two. These folks have a few more challenges to face surviving day to day than, say, the people that stayed here in the fifties and sixties."

"I've heard a lot about the Blue Onion from old-timers who used to cruise this stretch. What was it like?"

"It was your typical fifties-style drive-in. It was pretty traditional. You drove up and parked diagonally and the waitress came out in her little blue shorts and blue top and put the tray in the window—root beer, cheeseburgers, or whatever. It was a gathering place for teenagers."

"Was it affiliated with the motel?"

"It was built by the same company, Sierra Construction. At some point the businesses may have separated, but originally they were all tied together. The motel advertised that it had a restaurant and drive-in."

"What happened to the restaurant and drive-in?"

"They went the way of a lot of Fremont Street, where they stopped being the focal point, where kids didn't go to drive-ins, and there were more restaurants to go to in different parts of town. The town moved away from Fremont Street. The town moved to the northwest. The town moved to the south. They became isolated down here."

As we started west on Fremont, into a gantlet of tire shops, mini-marts, and weekly motels, I could sense the isolation. It was midafternoon, but it felt like midnight. The street was deserted and we shared the sidewalk with a woman wearing a halter top, microskirt, and high heels, who was clutching a can of beer. It was tough to tell which businesses were open and which were closed.

It was as if we were walking in a graveyard blooming with neon headstones.

"What was this stretch like in its prime?" I asked.

"Fremont Street was the first road Las Vegans used to get to Los Angeles. You would drive down Fremont and head toward Searchlight, so there was always a sense of energy here. In the mid-twenties, you could save sixty or seventy miles by using what's now Las Vegas Boulevard to get to L.A. But even then, the prospect of the dam being built kept this stretch of road alive. This is where you had the motels and various other businesses. The first string of car lots was on east Fremont. The retail outlets, like Sears and JCPenney, were farther up the street. The railroad depot was at the far end.

"This was a beehive of activity."

Fremont Street was the first paved road in Las Vegas. Nevada's first gambling license was issued to the Northern Club at 15 Fremont. The street featured the city's first air-conditioned casino (the Apache), first carpeted casino (the Horseshoe), and first high-rise building (the Fremont).

Now, it's the second most-famous street in Vegas ... and the last place you'd want to be.

"You mentioned that you used to cruise this area in high school," I said, as the Purple Sage's sign ("Family Units") came into focus. "What was the route and what was it like?"

"When I first came to town with my dad, we lived in the northwest. After about a year, I decided to move out on my own and live down here close to school, which was about nine or ten blocks west of where we are now. I rented a place on Bruce Street, so I'd come out on Bruce, head east on Fremont, and start at the Blue Onion. All the kids from Las Vegas High hung out there. It was new then."

"Yeah, the Blue Onion opened in nineteen fifty-six."

"Right. So it opened and the Blue Angel opened and that was a really hot place. And since it was close to where I lived, I'd start there. Then we'd drive up Charleston to Las Vegas Boulevard, which was Fifth Street, and make a left on Fremont. We'd drive to the depot and come back down Fremont. It was a social function. Most of the activity would take place from Main Street to Fifth and from Bruce to the Blue Angel. There were stoplights every block and we'd make sure to get caught at one of the lights, so we could interact with whoever was around."

I laughed. "What'd you drive?"

"A nineteen fifty-two DeSoto. It was a yellow hardtop coupe."

Smiling, I squinted into the sunlight. A school bus idled on the side of the street, in front of the Bonanza Lodge: "Wkly Rate$ Swim Area." The bus door opened and a boy in a backpack spilled out and disappeared into the motel's driveway.

When the bus pulled away, Bob and I could see the Fremont Street Experience on the horizon.

"I still haven't forgiven the city for taking the heartbeat out of Fremont Street," he said. "The idea of blocking off Fremont and creating a gambling mall—that was ludicrous. Now you can't turn from Las Vegas Boulevard, the iconic street in our community, onto Fremont. You can't drive up and down Fremont, like we used to do. That was the lifeblood of the street. In a lot of ways, that has hurt the eastern part of the street."

"How?"

"From the main gambling area on Fremont, you can't drive down here. You've got to go all the way around the Fremont Street Experience, so it has further isolated this area."

At Bruce, Bob and I crossed Fremont and started back toward the Blue Angel on the north side of the street. We passed a vacant lot littered with dead pigeons. A man in a floppy hat pushed a grocery cart down a side street.

"If you're by yourself and you let your mind wander, what do you think about when you drive this stretch now?"

"Oh, I tend not to be nostalgic. I tend to think of things more in their place in history and their potential for the future. I mean, when

I drive past the Blue Angel, I don't think of the times we partied there or had food fights or fistfights or any of those kind of things. I think about the opportunities. The Fremont Street Experience is twelve blocks from here. The Strip's just to the south. Boulder Highway is right down the street. There's got to be a way to make the magic happen here again. I think there just needs to be somebody with vision to take advantage of the opportunities that are here."

We walked under the Safari sign ("Daily Weekly Cable TV"), Sky Ranch sign (blank), and Roulette sign ("Weekly Monthly Laundromat").

"Also, I see the wonderful art of the neon in front of these motels and I say, 'We've got to save that.' We've got to preserve that history, so folks can understand what this part of Las Vegas was all about for a long time."

"Yeah," I said, looking up at pastel colors, cursive fonts, and kitschy images. "The signs are artistic."

"The Sky Ranch and Roulette signs are historic artifacts that need to be saved. They're two of the motels that have survived, that still have some energy. Maybe the signs, even though they don't light up anymore, are what's keeping them alive."

We passed a mini-mart and approached an auto-parts store.

"What do you see as the future of east Fremont?"

"Well, if I had my way, there would be a two-block area where we'd preserve the Sky Ranch and Roulette motels and a couple of others. There's half a dozen motels down here that really represent the traditional architecture of the forties and fifties, where they're shaped like an L or a U from the sky and the manager's office is up front. Those are truly pieces of history."

Bob and I stood on the curb, which was blackened by exhaust, and looked both ways. Cars flashed by on Eastern, but Fremont was clear. Sweating through our shirts, we crossed the street and stumbled under one of the arches.

"What would you do with the Blue Angel?" I asked, as we began back across the parking lot.

"It's still alive and well. It's alive and well, under these different circumstances. You've got a nightclub here that's open where the restaurant used to be." He pointed toward Club 2100, a squat stucco building that shares the parking lot with the Blue Angel.

"It's open on weekends," I said.

"What kind of club is it?"

"Hispanic."

"Well, to talk about preserving the Blue Angel or my favorite motels on the north side of the street is to ignore another force: the Hispanic community. Las Vegas is becoming more Hispanic and this is generally a Hispanic area. That culture could be part of the street's future, as well, whether it's nightclubs, stores, hotels, or motels. I mean, look at some of the places in Los Angeles and San Diego that are a mixture of a tourist attraction and Hispanic culture. Maybe that's the answer."

We glanced at the angel and continued toward the pool. Mack announced our return. Finally, we stopped in the shade of the breezeway, which was 20 degrees cooler than the parking lot. Bob's Benz—hubcaps gleaming in the half-light—was where he left it.

"Thanks for the tour," I said, shaking his hand. "Anything else we should know about the Blue Angel or east Fremont Street?"

"Well, we did see four or five young ladies of the night—or more accurately, older ladies of night—plying their trade. And yes, we saw other folks just trying to survive on the street. But we also found everyday human beings coming out of mom-and-pop stores or going into tire shops. We found historic buildings and signs worthy of preservation. This is not a barren war zone. This is still an area with energy and potential. You've got to walk the street to really see that. A drive-by observation just doesn't cut it on east Fremont."

WEDNESDAY

Don't stare. Don't ask questions. Don't stand out.

These rules weren't on the piece of paper I signed, but they're understood at the Blue Angel and other weekly motels on Fremont Street and Las Vegas Boulevard. If you follow them, you should be fine. If you don't, your door could be kicked in at four in the morning or a rock could fly through the window or the room could be torched. It's amazing what a match and a little gasoline can do to an old motel.

On Monday and Tuesday, I followed these rules. Now it was time to break them. I opened the door, dragged a chair onto the walkway, and began to read the morning paper. In this setting, the headlines ("Latina tapped for high court," "Three U.S. troops die in suicide blast," "Economists see recession ending this year") seemed less dramatic, the stories less significant. The NASDAQ, Dow Jones, and baseball and basketball box scores were a joke. Only the obits and job ads resonated.

Over the paper, I saw two men carrying coolers and wearing T-shirts, jeans, and dusty boots climb into a pickup truck ... a sun-burned scrapper stick his nose in the Dumpster ... a pasty woman in drugstore shades walk her dog to the pool, unleash it, and smoke as it squatted on the gravel and chased pigeons. The angel turned clock-wise; that's how time is measured at this motel.

Sam Gay, sheriff of Clark County from 1911 to 1931, used to sit on a bench on Fremont Street and look out at the saloons, casinos, cathouses, and train station. No need to chase the bad guys, he'd say. They all pass by here sooner or later. Leaning back in the chair, I wondered if Sheriff Doug Gillespie could sit on this end of Fremont and say the same thing.

I heard metal tapping against the blacktop, then a man emerged from the breezeway. Using a cane, he limped to the dumpster, emp-tied a trash can, and started back toward the shadows. He was six-foot-three and had a paunch. He was wearing a military baseball cap, a collared shirt, jeans, and black Velcro sneakers. I waved and he waved back.

"Were you in the military?" I said, as he neared the breezeway.

"I was on an aircraft carrier from sixty-six to sixty-eight in Viet-nam. I went right from high school into the Navy."

"I was thinking about you vets the day I checked in, Memorial

Day. I figured a few of you were staying here. Vietnam, huh?"

"Fifty-eight-thousand-plus men died over there. On the wall in Washington, D.C., there's over fifty-eight thousand names."

"That's a lot of people. We tend to forget how many soldiers died in Vietnam."

"And Korea."

"And Iraq and Afghanistan." I held up the paper. "I just read that five thousand soldiers have died over there."

"That's nothing. That's how many people died in my first six months in Vietnam."

He set the trash can down and leaned against a column in the breezeway. Removing the cap, revealing matted hair that was brown on top and gray on the sides, he wiped his brow and adjusted his prescription glasses.

"How long have you lived at the Blue Angel?" I said.

"About six months."

"How'd you come across this place?"

"I was looking for any place that was cheap, and I had just enough money to get the room, so I moved in. At first, I lived on the back side of the motel in a smaller room. Now I'm in one-thirty-three." He aimed his cane into the shadows.

"I'm in one-twenty-four," I said, pointing at the open door.

"What's your story?"

"I'm a writer. I'm just getting away from my apartment for a week. I figured I'd stay here and explore the neighborhood and look for inspiration and people to interview. You interested?"

He shrugged. "Sure."

"You want to do it now or later?"

"Let's do it this afternoon. Drop by my room around two or three."

"Room one-thirty-three?"

"Yep."

"What's your name?" I said, rising from the chair.

"Steve."

"I'm Matt," I said, shaking his hand. "I'll see you around two or three."

Steve's room backed up against mine and had the same floor plan and furniture—and the same smoky smell. A fan straddled the border of the main room and bathroom, exhaling 80-degree air. A bottle of water stood on one of the nightstands, a loaf of bread on the other. Clothes piled high in the far corner and a baseball bat leaned against the near corner, behind the door.

Steve sat at the table and petted Dot, his six-year-old toy poodle. I sat across from them. In between us, on the table, were an ashtray, lighter, pack of Marlboro Ultra Lights, notebook, and tape recorder.

"What'd you think of the Blue Angel when you first saw it?" I began.

"It was just like any other dive in town. It's a place to hang your hat and go to bed. Dot and I didn't care. We just needed a place to get out of the heat and the cold, and we figured this was it."

"What's it like here?"

"I've seen everything. It's the street life—the best of it, the worst of it. The worst of it has stolen my cell phone. It's stolen my dignity. You see things around here that scare you. You see people getting mugged, but don't say nothing. You'll get killed. I seen a guy get mugged the other day in broad daylight. They took his wallet. They were going to take his shoes if I hadn't stopped them. Of course, I couldn't do much. All I did was yell at them.

"Strange world here. Lots of homeless people. They come to Las Vegas thinking they're going to make it big, strike it rich. They end up in a tent city on Main Street or at a place like the Blue Angel."

"What's the best of it?"

"Well, it beats being homeless. At least you got a roof over your head. You got a TV. You got air conditioning. It's better than being stuck out there in the heat and worrying that somebody's going to roll you, shoot you, or stab you. The best part of it is you're somewhat protected. When you got a room, it seems like nobody messes with you. They want to be your friend because you got cover. You got a safe haven to fall back on when you want to get away from the streets for a minute."

"Who lives at the Blue Angel?"

"Retired people. People on the go. People that don't know where they're going or what they're doing. People trying to get somewhere in life. People looking for work, donating blood to survive. I live off one check a month."

"What check is that?"

"A non-service pension check from the military," he said, setting Dot on the floor. "Nine hundred and eighty-five dollars." He tapped a cigarette from the pack, picked up the lighter, and flicked it.

"You were talking about the people here," I said.

"There's all kinds of people here," he said, exhaling. "Some of them stay a long time, some of them a short time. Some of them you don't even know are here until they come out of their room by accident and you happen to see them. There's a guy on the back side of the motel, he's a miser. He lives in his room. The only time he ever comes out is to pay the rent.

"Some of them are loud, others are quiet. Some of them are women of the night, others work day jobs. One guy I know sits in his room all day typing on his computer and handicapping horse races. A couple I know sees who they can sponge off of and make money for meth. Another guy works at Sam's Town in the liquor department. And another guy's a manager at the ampm store.

"It's sort of like Peyton Place. Things happen here that you don't hear about and things you do hear about you're not sure really happened. It's an unusual place. I wouldn't recommend it to anybody, but it's better than being on the streets. I wouldn't put him through that." He looked at Dot, who was curled at his feet. "He can't fend for himself. He's an inside dog."

"How long have you had him?"

"Since he was six months old."

"Where'd you get him?"

"I was taking care of an elderly man in Tennessee and he wanted to go into a nursing home and he couldn't take his pup with him, so he left him with me. Him and I have been together ever since. He's the only true friend I've got and he gives me unconditional love. He don't ask for anything in return, except be there and feed him. And

Steve and Dot

he eats before I do. I make sure of that."

"You from Tennessee?"

"No. Indiana. I grew up on a small farm. The celebrity from my hometown was Virgil 'Gus' Grissom, the astronaut. My father went to school with him. Grissom was one of the first astronauts. He was supposed to go to the moon, but he went the hard way. He died on the launch pad in sixty-seven."

"What's the name of the town?"

"Mitchell. It's south of Bloomington."

"Where'd you go from there?"

"Fort Wayne, Indiana, and then Vietnam."

"What was Nam like?"

"I was in the Naval Air. Attack Squadron VA-172 out of Cecil Field, Florida. I worked on the flight deck. It was like being in a trance for two years. It was a different world. I went to boot camp and they made me a petty officer in charge of a squad because I was in the Boy Scouts. They said, 'Anyone with Boy Scout experience, you're a squad leader.'" He laughed. "So I went to Vietnam, spent two years there, and got out. When I came home, people shunned me because I'd been in a war they didn't approve of—women and children getting killed. I was part of that and they didn't like it."

"Looking back on it, what do you think about the war?"

"I didn't know anything about what was going on over there. I never was into politics. But when I came home, I found out that what happened three to six months ago in Vietnam was fresh news here. I realized the people were being lied to. The military was lying to the people of the United States to try to make things look better than they were."

"What do you think about the wars in Iraq and Afghanistan?"

"They should've ended a long time ago. It's all about oil. Cheney and Bush. It's all about the almighty dollar."

"What were your thoughts on Memorial Day?"

"Food. I was starving. I didn't have any food and I got no money until Sunday. I'm broke till then."

"What'd you do that day?"

"It was just another day of the week. I didn't even know it was a holiday until I happened to see a sign on a business that was closed."

"What's your typical day like?"

"I get up in the morning, maybe take a few hits off a joint. It helps get rid of my headaches. At noon, if I need some money, I'll go over to SuperPawn and wash car windows in the parking lot. Evening time, I'll walk around and maybe take a buck or two and sit at a slot machine at the gas station just to have something to do. Otherwise, I don't spend any money on gambling and I never drink."

"What about drugs?"

"Once in a while I might do some coke."

"Crack?"

"Yeah. I got into coke when I lived in Florida, but I slacked off when I got here. Once in a while I might go get a couple hits, kick back, and watch TV."

"What do you watch when you're high?"

"'George Lopez,' 'Law & Order,' 'CSI.' I watch a couple movies a week. 'Cash Cab.' I like that show. It keeps me attuned to current and past events, so I'm not so stupid."

I laughed, then looked out the window. Cars blurred by on Charleston Boulevard. I looked around the room, which was 15 feet by 15 feet and had beige cinder-block walls. An Indian-print blanket covered the bed and, beneath the sink, newspapers covered Dot's bed. Finally, I looked at Steve. Through a veil of smoke, I found his eyes— the left one green, the right one blue. "What'd you do when you got out of the military?"

"Well, I met a girl I thought was very interesting and appealing. Size four. She caught my eye. But she was married and her husband treated her really bad, so I beat him up and won her heart. She had two kids and was pregnant with my son. We got married. On the day of the wedding, I forgot the marriage license at her mom's house."

"That seems like a bad omen."

"It was. That was the first one. The second one was the minister said her name wrong. And bad omen number three was her mom and my mom wouldn't help us with the money we needed."

"What happened in the end?"

"I took the till at the place I was working at. She had two kids and my kid in the oven and we needed rent money and food money. We were in cahoots, but I turned myself in so she wouldn't lose the kids. I was looking at one to ten in the state pen, but my father knew the judge, so I got probation. Her and I, we broke apart after that. We just couldn't work it out."

"Where was this?"

"Fort Wayne, Indiana."

"Did you all have any other kids?"

"Yeah. She got pregnant again. Every time I looked at her she got pregnant. We have a daughter, too."

"What's your relationship like with your kids?"

"I never got to raise them or see them much or nothing."

"Why?"

"My ex-wife and my mom thought I was a bad influence. I guess I was the black sheep of the family. One thing led to another and I just bought me a Ford T-Bird and started traveling the country after my probation was over."

"Where'd you go?"

"All the way to West Yellowstone, Montana. I worked summer stock theater there. I was a stagehand. There was two theaters in town and there was, like, twenty of us that lived in cabins and worked the theaters. People coming through town to visit the park would stop and see the plays. It was population two hundred and something, but over two million people a year would come through there."

"Where'd you go from there?"

"I lived in Hawaii for thirteen years. I worked at the Sheraton in the convention department. I worked there for two and a half years until I fell and hurt my back. And then I became a cab driver."

"What was Hawaii like?"

"I smoked all the pot I could. It had the best pot in the world and all the girls you wanted to see in bikinis on the beach. I met some celebrities. I worked as an artist on the sidewalks of Waikiki, drawing portraits."

"Were you on Oahu the whole time?"

"No. I went to Kauai. I lived in a treehouse with a bunch of hippies when I first got there, back by Sleeping Giant, where they filmed 'South Pacific.' The Board of Health kicked us out after a year and a half, because we were pissing and shitting in the river."

"What brought you back to the mainland?"

"Island fever. It's like a dog chasing its tale. Nowhere to go. After a while, I got bored. I came back here and traveled around a little bit more and ended up in Yuma, Arizona, working for the carnival. I painted scenery and ran some of the games and drove the employees from town to town. But after ten years, I quit and got into speed. I got hung up on it. I didn't have anything for myself anymore. I'd given up on life.

"Then at the end of all that, I reunited with my ex-wife, who I hadn't seen in thirty years, in Florida."

"Really?"

"Yeah. It was like a honeymoon the first night. The second night was like, 'Your room's over there and my room's over here and give me your check every month and maybe you'll get to see your kids.'"

"Did you get to see them?"

"About two years later. She was in touch with them the whole time, but I didn't get to see them. Finally, when I did get to meet them, I saw that my boy looked just like me."

He reached into his back pocket, removed his wallet, and fished a plastic photo album from the well. Holding up the album, he flipped through it. His son and daughter came alive in the smoky sunlight. Blond hair, blue eyes, fair skin. Forced smiles, out-of-style clothes, yellowed photo paper.

"My daughter's thirty-three years old," he said. "She's got two kids. I'm a grandfather now."

"What about your son?"

"He chewed my ass out for not being there. I listened to him for over an hour. When I saw him, I hugged him. But then I just sat back and listened."

"He let you have it, huh?"

"Right between the eyes." He held his thumb and index finger an inch apart. "I felt about that tall. It hurt. We talked a few times after that, but we haven't been in communication since."

He stubbed his cigarette in the ashtray. I checked the recorder to make sure it was rolling. Dot stood and stretched, then disappeared into the bathroom.

"So bring it back around for me," I said. "How'd you end up in Vegas?"

"My ex-wife kicked me to the curb, just like she'd done before. I was right back where I started thirty-five years ago—with nothing. I went back to Yuma and stayed with a friend, but we couldn't get along. So I came here in November and that's when I found the Blue Angel. I saw the angel up there and said, 'Well, I guess God wants me to stay here.'"

"The sculpture above the motel?"

"Yeah. That's what attracted me to the place. They say that angels are watching over you; I figured that's the angel watching over

me. When I go out, that's the first thing I look at. When I come back, it's the last thing I see. She's always there. That's what's nice about it."

"She's watched over you?"

"I'm still alive, aren't I? I've beaten death at least once since I've been here. About three or four months ago, I coughed so hard I busted open inside and bled a couple pints in my stomach area. I was in the hospital for over a week. They'd come in every three hours and shoot me full of morphine, because I was hurting so bad."

He opened the bottom drawer of the nightstand and removed a list of doctor's appointments, including 11 in the next three months. Then he reached behind his chair and opened an art-supply box full of medicine.

"I'm on blood thinners for my blood clots. I have eyedrops for my glaucoma. I'm on seven or eight different kinds of pills for cholesterol. I'm on Xanax to try to make me forget the war. I've been on morphine for more than a year for pain. I got an inhaler for emphysema and asthma; I take two shots from it three times a day.

"When I came here, I was looking for a place to die and didn't even know it. So yeah, she's watched over me."

"What does she mean to you?"

"She's sort of like a helping hand. I look up and know that God's put her there for a reason: to watch over the people here, who are wayward, who are like ships in a storm. They dock in the harbor to get out of the weather and then they're off again. This place is like a port in a storm. Sometimes you stay overnight. Sometimes you stay a long, long time."

"How long are you going to stay?"

"Long enough to get healthy and then I'm moving on. I want to get out of this town. I don't really like it here."

"When you leave, what will you remember about the Blue Angel?"

"It was a stepping stone in the direction I wanted to go in, but I won't miss it. The only thing I'll miss is the angel.

"But God will have one watching over me wherever I go."

THURSDAY

She was leaning against a column in the breezeway, wearing an olive-green tank top, a lime-green floral-print skirt, and gold wedges. Her hair was red-brown and touched her shoulders, which were tan. A sequined handbag hung at her side.

As I approached from Charleston, she looked up from her cell phone. Her eyes were brown and she was wearing Hello Kitty earrings.

"You lost?" she said.

"No more than anyone else around here." I smiled and she smiled back. "I was supposed to meet someone at Carl's Jr., but she stood me up. Story of my life. Anyway, I was just looking around for her."

"She your girlfriend or something?"

"No. Just someone I was going to interview. Someone I wanted to talk to."

I explained I was a writer staying at the Blue Angel and I was looking for people to interview. I then invited her to dinner. She looked around, stuffed the phone in the handbag, and said, "Why not?"

She plucked a 22-ounce can of Bud Ice, sheathed in a paper bag, from the base of the column and we crossed the parking lot—the angel watching—and started west on Fremont. The sky was purple, the horizon orange. When she spoke, her tongue ring danced in the dying daylight. Two women in skirts and high heels waved to her from the other side of the street. Cars slowed and drivers leered. Even a drunk curled on a cardboard mat acknowledged her with a knit-capped nod.

I felt like I was walking the Mall with the queen.

She tossed the beer can into a dumpster and we disappeared into Odyssey Pizza. After ordering two Diet Cokes and a medium cheese pizza at the counter, we sat in a corner booth. As the neon signs blinked on and a parade of silhouettes marched past the window, she told me her story:

My name is Lisa, but some people call me Lacy. I'll be 50 years old next month. I live in room 226 of the Blue Angel with a guy named Dave, who I met two weeks ago.

For the record, Dave and I are just friends. It's platonic. I like him, but he needs to go out and have a good time. He needs to loosen up. For real. And he needs to make some decisions about what he's going to do with his life, instead of hem-hawing around. People come to Las Vegas thinking it's the land of opportunity, and then when things aren't handed to them on a silver platter, they can't figure out what to do. Opportunity isn't going to knock on your door. You have to go out there and find it.

When I moved into the Blue Angel, I was staying with a guy named BJ. He sells ShamWows, those spongy things that are really absorbent, at the swap meet. I met him at a bus stop—I didn't know him from Adam—and he wanted a roommate to split the rent with, because he's on a fixed income. But a week after I moved in, he said he was moving. So I had to get out of the room; I couldn't afford the rent on my own. That's when I met Dave and he said, "You can crash in my room until you get on your feet and find a place to stay."

The first time I ever heard of the Blue Angel, as far as I can remember, was when I met this guy walking down the street and we came back to his room to hang out. The room was trashed. I don't want to be crass, but he was an old drunk. We spent an hour or so drinking, then he started to get violent and told me to leave. I walked one door over and it was open and this guy was sitting there, so I said, "What's up with your neighbor? Why's he so crazy?" He said, "I don't know. That's just how he is, but don't let it bother you. Come on in."

Turns out the guy's name is Paul and he's a musician. He played the guitar for me. We watched a movie, "Across the Universe," based on the music of the Beatles. I immediately liked Paul; he's my cup of tea. But I wasn't looking for a boyfriend at the time. I'm not, like, looking for relationships. So he said,

"Come back whenever you want. If you need a place to stay, you can always stay with me."

Paul moved out, but I've been coming back to the Blue Angel ever since.

．　．　．

So you probably want to know a little bit about my background. Where I was born, where I was raised, that kind of stuff.

I was born in Santa Monica, California, and grew up in the San Fernando Valley. My parents were like Ozzie and Harriet. For real. They were married 38 years and never fought. They were strict, loving, and sweet. They really were. My sister and I had a great upbringing; we never went without. But I didn't realize that until I grew up and had kids of my own.

My mother was a stay-at-home mom. She was Italian. You never left the house without a plate of food and she always had gifts waiting for you if you were a guest. My father drove a bus for over 30 years.

I was my dad's favorite. No doubt about it. He used to always call me "baby" and I could get away with anything. He was a great dad. Perfect, really. It's sad in a sense, because women always look for men who are like their father. When you have a father like that, he's really hard to replace. To find a guy who's like my dad is nearly impossible, especially in this town.

Like I said, I'm a valley girl. I had a really good upbringing, but I was a rebel. I joined Greenpeace when I was six years old. I saved my lunch money to buy the "Beatles '65" album when it came out. And I wore an MIA bracelet when I was still in grade school.

You'll get a kick out of this: I wanted to be a journalist. Funny, huh? Bet you never would've guessed it. But at the time, there was so much going on and, having strict parents, I thought it would be a good way to be a part of it all. I had a high IQ and grade-point average. School was boring to me, so I'd get sidetracked by things like music, politics, and the environment.

I was 10 and there were hippies everywhere. I wasn't a grown-up, but I felt like one. I wanted to change the world.

. . .

When I was 13 or 14, I moved to Las Vegas—we had family here—and went to Chaparral High. I wrote for the school annual and newspaper. Chaparral has a vocational curriculum, which I thought would be perfect for me.

But then a bunch of stuff happened here and I moved back to California. Just personal things with my family. I don't want to talk about it. I don't know you that well. I mean, Jesus, we just met.

Anyway, I went back to California, fell in love, and married young. I have a 31-year-old son, a 26-year-old daughter, and a 16-year-old daughter. I hardly ever talk to my son and older daughter. They have their own lives and don't approve of my lifestyle. My 16-year-old's a Mini-Me and needs a mom. She lives with her dad, because I was unstable when she was starting school. She was supposed to come back and live with me at some point, but it just didn't work out that way. You know how that goes. Once your kids are gone, they're gone for good.

I feel bad about my relationship with my kids. I really do. I want to be a mom, but I can't. You can't make the sky orange when it's blue. You can't make somebody love you who doesn't love you.

I should know. I've been married three times. My older kids are from my first marriage and the youngest is from my second. The first marriage ended because there was no room for growth in the relationship. My husband didn't want me to go to school; he didn't want me to work; he didn't want me to grow as a person. Getting married in your teens is ridiculous anyway. I couldn't be a stay-at-home mom and not have any extracurricular activities. I'm just not like that. I'm not.

The second marriage ended because my husband was very erratic. He was moody, and I just can't deal with that.

The third marriage was secret and I don't really want to talk about it. It's none of your business anyway.

. . .

I don't miss my ex-husbands, but I miss my kids. They've either got their own lives and don't have time for their mother or they're embarrassed by me, which I don't understand. They weren't raised that way—and there's nothing that crazy about my lifestyle. I'm not a drug addict; I party, but I don't let it take over my life. I like to gamble—I'm lucky—but I'm not addicted to it. And yeah, I like to drink; a lot of people in Vegas do. But I'm not out of control.

And no, I'm not a prostitute. I just like to dress up. Just because I live on Fremont Street doesn't mean I have to wear a T-shirt, shorts, and flip-flops. If I was a hooker, why would I be on Fremont? I mean, come on. I don't think I'm all that, but I'd at least be on the Strip or working for an escort service or something.

I get propositioned all the time. Men pull up in their car and roll down the window and say, "You want a ride? You want a date?" Sometimes I'll catch a ride and tell them straight up, "I'm not a prostitute!" Then they try to talk me into it and I'm like, "You can let me out right here." But I've actually met some pretty cool people who have given me rides. I just like to meet people. I'm a people person.

So how do I survive? Friends. Like Ringo said, "I get by with a little help from my friends. I get high with a little help from my friends." I've always been resourceful. I'm not the type of person to just sit around and do nothing. I've worked. I've done fundraising. I've done telemarketing. I've booked bands and helped manage them and stuff like that.

But to be honest with you, I don't think I should have to work. I'm a gypsy. When I was living in California, I moved eight times in six months. I've lived in Scottsdale, Arizona, and Bremerton, Washington. I've lived in national parks and in small towns that had more bears than people. I've lived on the beach in Ventura. I've been in Las Vegas the last year or so, but I've jumped around a lot here.

So far, this is my favorite neighborhood. It's a magnet. There's always people out and about. There's always something going on. You can go to the Strip on, like, a Wednesday night and it can be dead. There'll hardly be anyone around. But Fremont Street's always got action.

I like the action. I don't feel threatened by it. A lot of people think it's scary, but I get along with everyone. They're always like, "What's happening, girl? How's it going? Come over here. Talk to me. You want to get a drink? You want to party?"

That angel above the motel's also a magnet. She pulls people in. She's unique. I think she moves on her own—no wind, motor, or nothing. I believe she's a real angel. I believe in angels. I believe in ghosts. I believe in spirits. There's something spiritual about her. Sometimes she moves when there's no wind at all. Not a trace. She'll turn and turn and then stop and look dead at you. It's a trip. It makes you wonder if you've done something good ... or something bad.

.   .   .

I like the Blue Angel. I wish it had more foliage and there was water in the pool. And sometimes it seems like there's a lot of angry people there. A few nights ago, a couple fights broke out. They may have been drug-related. You know how that goes. And you have homeless people who hang out in the breezeway and sell stuff and you don't know if it's been stolen or what. I'm used to all that, though. I mean, not everybody goes to the top of the Stratosphere every night and has lobster. Not everybody's born with a silver spoon in their mouth.

But if you live at the Blue Angel, people assume you're a prostitute or a crackhead or you just can't get your act together. That's not the case. People live there for a variety of reasons. One older gentleman I know honeymooned there and lives there because of that memory. Another man I know is saving money. I just like old eccentric places. I'm not saying I don't like to live in the lap of luxury, but it will do for now.

I don't know this for sure, but I bet a lot of musicians have stayed at the Blue Angel. I can see them driving into town in a van and needing a place to stay and ending up there. Or maybe their manager put them up there, because it was cheap.

Maybe the Beatles stayed there. Or one of the Beatles. Maybe George. He's my favorite Beatle, because he was different—and he turned out to be a hippie, too. I don't know. I was just always drawn to George for some reason. He was my kind of guy.

I bet some writers have stayed there, too. You're not the first one. Not by a long shot.

My favorite writer's Thoreau. He's political, but also personal. It's heavy stuff. Very emotional. It doesn't make sense to a lot of people, but I understand it. I can relate to it.

Like Thoreau, I like to be independent. I wish I had my own Walden, my own sanctuary. I've always wanted to live on an island that nobody could visit without my permission. It'd be the best place on Earth. For real. I'd allow musicians and artists on it, certain family members, friends. I'd be in control for once. I'd finally be able to tell someone, "Get out of my face! Stop breathing my air!"

If I can't have my own island, I want a church. That's one of my dreams: to live in a church, so the demons can't get me.

.   .   .

An island, church, or wherever, I'll be leaving the Blue Angel soon. It's time for me to go. I can sense it. I can feel it coming, like the seasons.

I won't forget the Blue Angel, though. That's for sure. I'll remember it as part of an interesting and difficult time in my life, but I try to learn from all my experiences. I believe I'm put in a place for a reason. I don't know what that reason is sometimes, but I still believe that. I walk by faith and not by sight. I'm biblical. You might not believe it, but I've read the Bible front to back. I've got a Bible and rosary beads in my room right now. Galatians 5:22: "But the fruit of the Spirit is love, joy, peace, longsuffering, kindness, goodness, faithfulness." 5:23: "Against such there is no law." In other words, as long as you love and are peaceful and you suffer, you're going to be all right. In that case, I know I'm going to heaven.

But I don't know where I'm going next. There's no telling. I live day to day. Whatever opportunity comes my way, I'm going to go for it. One thing I've learned is you have to seize the moment. Carpe diem. There's no time to think about it. You have to trust your intuition, because that moment may never come again. It could be anything: a job, a good time, a new friend. The possibilities are endless.

In the meantime, I'll just go where the next ride takes me.

FRIDAY

Throughout the week, I observed the angel like an astronomer observing a planet.

When I woke, I rubbed the sleep from my eyes, opened the curtain, and squinted up at the angel. I stopped and stood beneath her on my way to Denny's, McDonald's, Chinatown Cuisine, ampm, or CVS. Before crawling into bed and watching a movie on my laptop, I cracked the curtain and said, "Good night."

I studied her surface (curved and rippled), composition (fiberglass exterior, steel axis, hollow interior), and distance from Earth (45 feet), but I was obsessed with her rotation. She turned clockwise and counterclockwise, patiently and impatiently, seemingly with purpose and without. Monday night, she faced east. Tuesday afternoon, she faced north. Thursday evening, she watched the sun set. I'd not seen her even glance south … until this morning.

As I leaned against the windowsill, looking through my high-haired, slit-eyed, and pale-faced reflection, the angel turned and turned and then stopped and looked at me. My eyes opened and I cracked a smile. I finally felt welcome at the Blue Angel. I finally felt that the angel was watching over me, too.

An hour later, my cell phone rang. It was Betty Willis, who designed the "Welcome to Fabulous Las Vegas" sign and the Blue Angel sign and sculpture. Thanking her for returning my call, I sat at the table.

"I'm in room one-twenty-four of the Blue Angel," I said, "looking out the window at the sculpture you designed. It's beautiful."

"Well," said Willis, calling from her home in Overton, Nevada, "a lot of it was the work of the company that made it. I did an approximate sketch and they took it from there."

"What company was that?"

"I don't remember. That was when I was a kid. In other words, that was a *long* time ago."

"How old are you now?"

"Eighty-six. You know what that means? Eight miles out and six feet under. That's what the gangsters used to say."

I laughed. "What inspired you to create the angel?"

"I'd done a lot of ads for the casinos and drawings of dancing girls and columns, so I drew her and put her on a pedestal. I had little bluebirds circling around and carrying a ribbon up to drape over the pedestal. She rotated so that the wand went around and blessed the motel and neighborhood."

"Was she modeled on anyone in particular?"

"No. I just drew what I thought an angel would look like. She'd be in a full gown and have long blond hair and a halo. And I got a lot of flak for it."

"What do you mean?"

"People complained that I made her boobs too big. They said an angel wouldn't have boobs like that. I said, 'Well, bring me an angel and I'll fix them.' They never did find one, so I never did fix them."

"Who complained? Locals or tourists?"

"I don't know. I don't remember. I just remember I was criticized for the way I drew her. I don't remember her breasts being that big, but I do remember they were a *big* problem."

"That's ridiculous. This is Las Vegas. Everyone here has big breasts."

She laughed. "It was an accident. I never meant for her breasts to be big. They just turned out that way. So what?"

I looked at the angel. "The breasts are still there, but the blue-birds are gone."

"They were smaller units of glass, which are difficult to keep burning," said Willis, who was born in Overton and raised in Las Vegas. "Small units of glass burn out quickly."

"They've been replaced by pigeons."

"Great. That's the problem with signs; pigeons get in them and screw up the wiring. I've known sign people who've tied their wings behind them and dropped them off the top of hotels. I never did think that was very nice, but keeping the signs clean and working is a con-stant battle."

"The angel looks good."

"The sign company probably keeps her clean; they have a main-tenance program. Or maybe the motel cleans her up every once in a while."

"The sign beneath the angel *doesn't* look so good. You designed that, too, right?"

"Yeah. Back then there were only, like, fifty letter styles and you had to buy them for a hundred and fifty bucks apiece, so we didn't get too creative. Before you used a font, you had to really think about it. Now there are hundreds of fonts. You can get them for free and the computer cuts out the letter exactly as it is. Every font in the world is at your beck and call."

"I like the font you used. It's cool. Very curvy."

"The top of the 'M' is curved and so is the back of the 'E.'"

"What style's that?"

"Who knows? That was done before they had names for fonts. It's Betty Willis style, I guess. It's like when people ask me about that sign on the Strip and where I got the word 'Fabulous' from. Out of my head."

I shifted in the seat. "I wasn't going to bring up the 'Welcome to Fabulous Las Vegas' sign. You must get sick of talking about it."

"They got upset when I didn't go to the fiftieth reunion," said Willis of the sign, which debuted in 1959. "I probably should've gone, but it's hard. I would've had to have somebody help me get dressed and pin my hair down, so it doesn't blow around. Somebody would've had to drive me to Las Vegas and hold me up or unload a wheelchair. It's a lot of work and I don't like imposing. When I lived in town, it was a little easier.

"People always want me to pose in front of that sign with a bunch of showgirls or something, and it gets to be a burden."

"They would've sent a limo to pick you up for that event."

"I don't know. Anyway, that sign can stand on its own. It doesn't need me around anymore."

Again, I looked at the angel. And she was looking at me, as if listening to the conversation. "Enough about the 'Welcome' sign. What do you remember about designing the Blue Angel sign and sculpture?"

"We used a company in California that made models for shop windows. They took on the project, which was big for them." She paused. "I'm trying to think. That sound you hear is my brain working." Silence. "Then two men in Las Vegas who did stuff for the shows finished it in their backyard; a lot of sign people worked on their patios back then. Plus, I don't think it could fit into a shop.

"But the main thing I remember is it became an eastern destination on the Fremont Street drag."

"You drew it on paper?"

"Yeah. Vellum paper. You'd do the drawing and lettering with a pencil, then run them through a blueprint machine. You'd show the customer some of the renderings. Then the renderings would be painted on a full-size piece of cardboard and fluorescent tubing would represent the neon. It was all done by hand."

"Who were you working for at the time?"

"In the forties, I worked freelance doing casino ads," said Willis, who went to art school in L.A. in 1942 and returned to Las Vegas in '45. "When I went into the sign business in the early fifties, I worked for Western Neon. Ted Rogich, [political consultant] Sig Rogich's father, worked there and was an ambitious salesman. He probably sold the Blue Angel sign."

"Then Young Electric Sign Company bought Western Neon?"

"Yeah. But nobody called me. I wasn't part of the sale. Finally, Ted told me there was a new sign company in town called AdArt, so I went and worked for them. They ended up doing or redoing most of the signs on the Strip. They completely changed the look of Las Vegas."

"The angel's bigger, stronger, and more masculine than the typical angel. Was that intentional?"

"No. That was probably just the mood I was in. And if I'd designed her on a computer—right before I retired, sign people started using computers—I would've just cut out one of the dancing girls I'd drawn and used her."

"She looks like a real woman, not a fantasy. Strong and tough. She's appropriate for the neighborhood."

"I understand the neighborhood has changed. I used to live right down the street from the Blue Angel. My mom had a beautiful home on Seventh and she sold it and we moved to Mayfair Circle, which is between Charleston and Fremont around Sixteenth Street. The area was nice then; my mom wouldn't have moved there if it wasn't. Now it's home to a different crowd, I guess. Oh well. It doesn't make any difference to me. I don't care what anybody does, as long as they're not hurting anyone. It's none of my business."

"At one time, the angel was powered by a motor. Now she's turned by the wind. When I woke up this morning, she turned and looked directly into my room. And she's still looking this way."

Betty laughed. "Well, I'll be darned. That must make you self-conscious."

"Actually, I finally feel welcome at the motel. The people here have a lot of respect for the angel. They say she watches over them."

"That's what she was designed to do. When the motor was working, she turned clockwise. She turned slowly, so the wand blessed the whole neighborhood."

"She cast quite a spell. In some ways, the neighborhood seems cursed."

"I'm sorry about that. I've sat and thought about what we can do to change things there, but I haven't come up with anything."

"Do you care about the motels your signs are in front of? Or is that none of your business?"

"My signs can't stop progress. The motel's going to turn into whatever it's going to turn into. The neighborhood's going to turn into whatever it's going to turn into. I designed the Moulin Rouge sign and it lit up the whole neighborhood, but the casino closed and the area went downhill. I also designed the Del Mar sign. It was an important motel in its time and it became a whorehouse."

"Yeah. It was an hourly motel when it closed."

"All of central Vegas, from what I understand, has gone downhill. It was beautiful. A lot of good people came from there. For instance, me."

I laughed and set my elbows on the table. "Like I said, the angel means a lot to the people who live here. What's that mean to you?"

"It means a lot," said Willis, who retired in 2000 and moved to Overton in '08. "You get so many complaints about your designs. When I was a sign designer, I taught a lettering class. I was teaching call-out lettering, a style that's fast and easy, and this one yokel says, 'Yeah, but would a professional use that style?' I said, 'I guess so. I've been using it for thirty years.'

"There's always someone on the sidelines who has something smart to say, so it means a lot to have those people say something nice about her."

"What's the strangest thing anyone's said to you about the angel?"

"Most people don't even know I designed her. It came as a shock to everybody when they found out I did the Moulin Rouge sign. I designed a lot of the old signs in Las Vegas. When I build them, they last."

"How long do you think the angel will last?"

"I expect all my signs to go down before I do. I'm a tough old bird. I'm not going until I'm ready."

"How does the Blue Angel sign compare to the 'Welcome' sign, the Moulin Rouge sign, and others you designed?"

"A lot of the signs I designed have changed. They've been added to and remodeled and so forth. But I designed quite a few that, in one way or another, stood out in their time. One thing I'm proud of is I did a lot of things that everybody else eventually copied.

"I had a baby and a mother to take care of and I used to stay up late to come up with designs and think of something that'd make them special. I spent a week in the library studying French lettering to find the right style for the Moulin Rouge sign. I'm proud of that. I'm proud that I was a forerunner in the business."

"Was there anything unique about the Blue Angel sign?"

"She was on a round column and the ribbon was pulled up by the bluebirds. That cost a lot of money to do. That was a *very* difficult neon job."

I leaned back and looked out the window. The angel turned slowly to the east. "Well, Mrs. Willis, I've kept you a long time. I just have one last question: Is there anything you want to say to the people at the Blue Angel?"

"Tell them that I guarantee the angel will stand as long as the motel does. And she is watching over them, whether it seems like it or not. Many times, we wonder about the things we have and don't have. I feel like I've been blessed with a long, interesting, and good life. And I wish the same for all of them."

SATURDAY

Seventy-eight degrees. Partly cloudy. A half-moon tilted like a beggar's cup. Mack was in the pool area, circling like a shark, barking, and clawing at the chain links. There was madness in the air—and he was the first to sense it.

Somewhere in the shadows, a woman was gasping and crying and screaming. Her voice echoed in the parking lot. Smelling blood, Mack stood on his hind legs and howled at the moon. I looked at the angel, assuming she'd finally broken down. After more than 50 years above the motel—all the beauty and ugliness, kindness and meanness, loyalty and betrayal, love and hate, and pleasure and pain—she'd finally flinched. I expected to find her kneeling on the pedestal, head buried in her arms, wings up ... the wand seesawing on the edge of the roof ... the halo spinning on the driveway.

It must get lonely up there, old girl. It must be hard, the hopes and dreams of the tenants resting on your broad but fragile shoulders. I know your secret: On hot days and cold nights, you consider jumping.

But the angel, silhouetted by the lights of weekly motels, low-stakes casinos, pawnshops, hubcap dealers, and payday loan stores, was on her perch, standing tall and waving the wand, just as Betty Willis drew her.

Cutting through the breezeway and looking across Charleston, I discovered the wailing was coming from the Iglesia Pentecostal Ministerios Leon de Juda, which was holding its service in the parking lot of a strip mall. A skinny woman with stringy black hair stood at the pulpit, mic tilted toward her. The angel was a study in restraint, the woman in emotion. She clutched her chest and winced, as if shot. I scanned the balcony of the Blue Angel for suspects. Four or five doors were open and tattooed brown-skinned men in tank tops leaned against the railing, holding beer cans, not rifles.

Wayne, who co-manages the motel with his wife Kerry, emerged from the breezeway. Wearing a baseball cap, T-shirt, jeans, and sneakers, and gripping a flashlight like a bludgeon, he looked west, then east.

"You working?" I asked.

"Yeah," said Wayne, head on a swivel.

"What's going on?"

"Some guy just punched out his girlfriend."

"You serious?"

"Yeah. We called the cops, but they haven't come yet."

"How long's it been?"

"A half-hour."

"That's ridiculous."

"I know," he said, shaking his head. "Saturday nights."

Wayne disappeared beneath the breezeway and I sat on the base of a column, waiting for the cops. A mustached man stood at the pulpit and strummed a Spanish guitar. The 206 squealed to a stop; people filed off and on. Emergency lights flashed at Charleston and Bruce and Charleston and Eastern (had the whole neighborhood gone mad?), but not at the Blue Angel.

Lisa's roommate Dave stepped out of the shadows, sat next to me, and lit a cigarette.

"I threw Lisa out today, man," he said, exhaling. "She's gone."

"What?"

"She scratched the shit out of my arm, so I got her eighty-sixed from here."

"What happened?"

"She's a nut, dude. She's psychotic. She needs to be on meds. I just couldn't handle it anymore."

"You kicked her out?"

"I'd been telling her for a while that she needed to find another place to stay. She was like, 'Oh, that's no problem. I got a hundred places I can stay. I got a hundred men that want me to live with them.' I said, 'Fine. Go live with them.' But she'd come back and I'd give her another chance to get her shit together. She'd say, 'I'm not going to drink anymore. I'm not going to stay out late.' As soon as it got dark, she was out there doing it again.

"So I called her this morning and said, 'You need to get your stuff out of my room.' She starts going off, 'Fuck you! You're a piece of shit! You're an asshole!' I said, 'Just get your stuff.' She wouldn't, so I called the cops and asked what I could do to get her out of my room. They said, 'When she shows up, call us and we'll escort her off the property.'

"She showed up with this guy and they were sitting at the bottom of the stairs drinking. The maid was cleaning my room, so I was outside and I could hear her talking about me, and the guy crushed his beer can, like he was going to do something. He started going into the room and I said, 'Don't come in my room, man!' Then I told Lisa, 'Get your stuff and leave.' She starts screaming, 'This is my room! I'm on the lease!' So I grabbed the receipt for the room—that's when she scratched me—took it to the manager, and said, 'I want her out of here!'"

He extended his arm, revealing six-inch scratch marks.

"Damn!" I said.

"I'll tell you what. It took everything I had not to throw her over the railing. I just went to the manager and said, 'Call the cops.'"

"They escorted her off the property?"

"Yep. They asked me if I wanted to press charges and I said, 'No.'"

"Where's she now?"

"I don't know and I don't care. She's not my problem anymore."

Dave—five-foot-ten and 160 pounds—stubbed the cigarette on the column, then flicked it onto the driveway. Shuffling his shell-toe sneakers and digging into the front pocket of his jeans, he removed a crumpled pack of Marlboros, tapped one out, and lit it.

"So what are your plans?" I said.

"I'm going back to Colorado," said Dave, shaved head and rectangular-frame glasses shining. "I'm leaving in two weeks, maybe sooner. I've got to find work. I called some people I know and they said there's work there, so I'm catching a Greyhound and getting the hell out of Dodge. I've had enough of this shit. Too many lowlife motherfuckers out here, man."

"How long you been in Vegas?"

"About two months."

"What brought you here?"

"I wanted to find a job, maybe a couple of them. Maybe meet some nice people, find a girlfriend. You know, settle down."

"What kind of work were you looking for?"

"I've worked in casinos. But I have a felony from twenty years ago, so I can't get a sheriff's card. I can't be a security guard, either. I can work in a restaurant. I can load trucks. I can do shipping and receiving. Stuff like that."

"You didn't find anything?"

"Nah. I didn't have any luck."

"How'd you come across this place?"

"I was talking to a guy on the street and I told him I was staying at the Siegel Suites. He said, 'Man, that place is expensive!' Then he told me about the Blue Angel, so I got my stuff and moved in."

"How long you been here?"

"A month."

"You going to miss anything about it?"

"The managers. I like them. People talk a lot of shit about them, but they do a good job. They've been good to me. Wayne got me a microwave oven and Kerry's been really nice to me, too."

"What about Lisa?"

He took a drag from the cigarette, then exhaled. "Yeah, I'm going to miss her, but not her bullshit. I'm not going to miss it at all.

"But honestly, she was one of the highlights of my stay. She's a fun girl. For a while, she was all right. I met her just like I'm talking to you now. She was sitting on a column crying and I walked up to her and asked what was wrong. She told me about her situation and I said she could stay with me for a few days, then get her own place.

"But she's also one of the reasons I want to leave. If I don't, I'm going to be stranded like all the other people around here. I mean, look at her. She's stuck. She's fifty years old and she's going to be running that same game until she's dead in a ditch."

A shiny black SUV turned into the driveway and eased through the breezeway. It swung around the island of palm trees, then parked in the lot shared by the Blue Angel and Club 2100. Above the rush of traffic, I could hear music thumping in the club.

"What are Saturday nights like around here?"

"It depends. They can be crazy and they can be calm. I usually stay in, watch TV, and relax. I try to stay out of trouble."

"What are you up to tonight?"

"I'll probably just go back to the room and watch TV. It'll be a boring night and a boring day tomorrow, then I'll try to hustle up a day or two of work before I leave town."

I stood and extended my hand. "I'm going to try to find Steve and see how he's doing. Best of luck, man."

"Thanks," said Dave, shaking my hand. "Good luck to you, too."

I curled around the column and knocked on Steve's door. No answer. Leaning to my left, I looked in the window and noticed a cardboard sign that read, "I'm at Pepe's & SuperPawn." I started east on Charleston.

At Eastern, fried beef and exhaust fumes fouling the air, I ran into Steve's friend Tom, who has lived at the Blue Angel for two months and donates blood twice a week to pay the rent.

"Some guy punched out his girlfriend," I said.

"Yeah, I know," said Tom, who's from Chicago. "I don't know the guy's name, but he lives upstairs with his girlfriend and mother. His girlfriend knocked on my door and she had a cut on her forehead and was crying. He did it right in front of the women that work in the office. They were like, 'You're out of here tomorrow morning!'"

"Where did it happen?"

"On the balcony above Charleston. The two women that work in the office were coming back from Albertsons with their groceries and saw the whole thing."

"In front of the church service?"

"Yeah. I heard the guy took off. His girlfriend told me they've had domestic violence issues before and if he got caught he'd go to jail and they'd put his mom in an old-folks home, because she's handicapped."

"And this afternoon, the cops escorted Lisa off the property. Is this a typical Saturday at the Blue Angel?"

"No. This is the first time I've seen two things like that happen on the same day. I've seen marshals come and take people from their rooms, because they had warrants. And a couple months ago, this guy that was dating a stripper that lived downstairs drove his truck under the breezeway—it barely fit—skidded out and got all up in her face. Then he got in Wayne's face and shoved him. Wayne was going to kick his ass and Mack was ready to jump the fence, but the guy took off."

"Do they put Mack in the pool area every Saturday night?"

"Yeah. They used to have an igloo house in there for him, but one morning we woke up and it was gone. Somebody stole it. I felt bad for the dog. I mean, what the fuck?"

"Yeah, that's cold."

We paused as an ambulance passed the Blue Angel and turned left on Eastern.

"Did you hear gunshots last night?" said Tom. "I thought I heard some."

"No. But my air conditioner's so loud, someone could get shot right in front of my door and I wouldn't hear it."

"How long did it take you to find the light switch that cuts on the AC?"

"About two hours. I was like, 'Fuck, they don't have AC!' It was burning up in there."

"Dude, I sat in my room for two weeks before I noticed that little switch. I'm not even joking."

I laughed, then looked down Charleston. "Is Steve at Pepe's and SuperPawn?"

"Yeah. He's down there."

"All right. I'm going to catch up with him. I'll catch you later, man."

"OK. Later, dude."

I continued east on Charleston. It was 10:30 p.m., but it felt like noon. The lanes were cluttered with cars and the area was bathed in light: neon signs, casino billboards, the flickering glow of the Fremont Street Experience. The pigeons seemed confused. They perched on the roof of a block-long strip mall (Hub Cap Annie, Cashworks, JV Tax Services) and pecked at the asphalt of the parking lot, a sure sign of a mad and sleepless neighborhood.

At the end of the strip mall, I saw Steve leaning on his cane in the parking lot shared by Pepe's and SuperPawn. A Hispanic man carrying a to-go box stopped, reached for his wallet, and handed him some money. As the man climbed into his car, I approached Steve.

"Is this your spot?"

"Yep. Pretty much."

"Don't let me interrupt. I just wanted to say hello."

"No problem."

I looked at his hand. "Did you make a score?"

"Two bucks. A little pocket change."

"How often are you here?"

"Every other night. I just try to make a little money, so I can eat dinner."

"How do you do?"

"I come here during the day and wash car windows, then I come back at night. I make ten, twenty, maybe thirty dollars. I can't work, so I might as well do something. I get bored sitting around the room all day watching TV."

"So what's new?"

"I went to the VA and they're going to help me get in HUD housing, so I don't have to spend half my check on rent. I'm supposed to go back and see them next week."

"How you feeling?"

He shook his head. "Blood clots. My leg's swollen and sore. It bugs me all the time. It's a pain you wouldn't believe. It's unbearable. Sometimes it feels like a hot needle hitting a nerve. And I'm having trouble seeing. That glaucoma destroyed my eye. I've had two surgeries on it already and it ain't getting any better."

"Get off that leg and let me buy you something to eat," I said, motioning toward Pepe's.

"I'm not hungry. Just get me a Coke, no ice."

I entered the restaurant, then returned with a Coke and Jamaica tea.

"One time," said Steve, "a guy came out of Pepe's and gave me two pennies. You can't knock it, I guess; every penny counts toward a taco or sandwich. Another guy gave me a handful of change, then came back and said, 'Let me see what I gave you.' He took all the silver back and left the copper. When he drove away, I threw the pennies at his car and said, 'If you need them that bad, take them!'"

I laughed. "What's the rudest thing anyone's done to you here?"

"This guy parked in front of SuperPawn and asked me to wash his windows. I said, 'Sure.' When he came out of the store, he walked right past me, got in his car, and drove away without giving me a cent. What a jerk! I felt like pissing on his car seat."

"Yeah, payback's a mother."

"But the Mexicans here are more generous than the white people. They give from the heart. They've really helped me and I have a lot of respect for them."

Sipping our drinks, Steve and I started back toward the Blue Angel. "I've been meaning to ask you something," I said. "The motel rules say no pets allowed, but a lot of tenants have cats or dogs. What's going on?"

"You got to pay a fee, twenty-five dollars a week, and they want you to clean up after your pet."

"Another rule says the maximum stay is twenty-eight days, but some tenants have been there for months."

"They make you move out, but you can move back in. That's what most people do."

We crossed Charleston at Eastern, then continued west. The church service had ended and the parking lot of the strip mall was dark. The balcony was deserted, the doors closed. The cops still hadn't arrived.

We stopped in the breezeway. Breathing heavily, Steve leaned against a column.

"I think I'm checking out tomorrow," I said.

"Really?"

"Yeah. I've had enough fun for one week."

"Too much excitement, huh?"

"No. It's been a good experience. It's just time for me to get back to my apartment and get some other things done. What are your plans?"

"I'm going to stay here and keep going to my doctor's appointments. They're trying to fix my leg—knee-replacement surgery—so I'm going to let them do that. It's going to take at least three months to recover. The first few weeks, you can't even get out of bed to go to the bathroom. That's how bad it's going to be."

"Let me know if I can help in any way."

"If I go to the hospital, you can bring me a crossword-puzzle book. Or a Louis L'Amour paperback. His Western novels are excellent. He's one of my favorite writers."

"No problem."

"And thanks for interviewing me for your book. Nobody's really asked me about my life before."

"Thanks for talking to me."

"Is it going to be softbound or hardbound?"

"I don't know. If I get a book deal, that'll be the publisher's decision."

"You going through New York?"

"I'll probably try a few bigger publishers and a few smaller ones. Depends how the book turns out."

"Right on," said Steve, straightening up.

"Cool, man," I said, shaking his hand. "Hopefully I'll see you tomorrow. If not, take care."

"I will. Good luck in your adventures."

"Good luck to you, too."

As Steve limped south, I started north. The parking lot was full and a line formed at the door of Club 2100. The half-moon balancing on her halo, the angel was facing the club and twisting in the wind, axis squeaking.

Returning to my room, I fastened the chain, turned the button on the handle, and threaded my pen through the eye of the sliding-bolt lock.

SUNDAY

As the sun threw the angel's shadow onto the parking lot and painted my room red, I balanced the laptop on the edge of the bed and
watched *Der Blaue Engel* (*The Blue Angel*).

The 1930 movie, considered the first major German talkie, stars
Emil Jannings as Immanuel Rath, a ruler-to-the-knuckles teacher who
discovers that some of his students frequent the Blue Angel cabaret.
Hoping to confront the students, Rath visits the Blue Angel and falls
in love with headliner Lola Lola, played by Marlene Dietrich. He re-
signs, marries Lola, and dedicates himself to her career, touring with
the troupe.

But Rath and Lola run out of money ... she becomes disinter-
ested ... and he's reduced to selling postcards of her at shows and
performing as a side act (a clown, appropriately). During a show at
the Blue Angel, where he's heckled by the patrons he once judged,

Rath snaps and attacks Lola. Regaining his senses—and realizing he's lost everything—he staggers back to his old school and collapses on his desk, clinging to it like a raft on an ocean.

There are a hundred Immanuel Raths at the Blue Angel Motel, I thought as the credits rolled. People who had successful careers, were seduced by a woman, drink, drug, or game of chance, and hit rock bottom. People who suffered precipitous falls and raw humiliation. People who snapped. The Blue Angel is their school, the bed their desk.

I, too, was Immanuel Rath. I strayed from my safe, simple, and regimented life and entered a world I'd only heard about in whispers, a world more human and complicated than I imagined. Would it seduce me? Would it humble me? Would it destroy me?

I closed the laptop, crawled out of bed, and stepped into the shower. Drying off and getting dressed, I began to pack. The Blue Angel is more depressing than dangerous, I thought as I stuffed my razor and gel into the shaving bag. It's easy to see why people kill themselves in Las Vegas weekly motels. If you're on stable ground, they push you to the edge. If you're on the edge, they push you over.

I didn't see any ghosts, I thought as I folded my shirts on the bed and placed them in the duffel bag, but the room is haunted. It's haunted by everyone who stayed in it before me. Who were these people? What brought them to Vegas? To east Fremont Street? To the Blue Angel? What were their hopes and dreams?

On six hours of sleep each of the last six nights (the room was never cooler than 80 degrees and the sheets were sticky), I couldn't answer these questions. There were too many years to cover. Too many people. Too many possibilities. Humming the theme song of *Der Blaue Engel*, which was stuck in my head, I unplugged the cellphone charger and sheathed the laptop in my workbag. I looked under the bed; nothing there. Picking up the bags, I stumbled to the door, pulled the pen from the lock, then exited.

The office door opened with a squeal, the bell rang, and Belinda (the redhead) appeared behind the Plexiglas, as if she'd never left. Slipping the key off my chain, I placed it in the tray.

"I'm checking out," I said.

"You have your receipt?"

I reached into the workbag and removed the receipt. She scooped it from the tray, scribbled on it, and slid it back to me with my $20 deposit.

"Sign at the bottom."

I signed with the pen chained to the counter. "Can you call a cab?"

"Yeah," she said, disappearing into the shadows. I heard a phone book flop open, her finger punch the keypad, and hold music. She reappeared.

"Interesting place you got here," I said, smiling.

She laughed. "Last night? Yeah, Saturdays are crazy. We have the club next door and a bunch of other stuff going on."

"She going to be all right?" I said, referring to the woman who was punched by her boyfriend.

"Yeah. She'll be all right."

Belinda turned her back to me and filed my paperwork in an accordion folder. The hold music seemed to get louder. It filled the room. Finally, it cut off and she picked up the receiver.

"I need to have somebody pick up a tenant. The Blue Angel Motel. Charleston and Eastern." She looked up. "Where you going?"

"Desert Inn and Paradise."

"DI and Paradise. Uh-huh. OK. Thank you." She hung up the phone. "They'll be here in twenty minutes."

"OK," I said. "I'll wait in the breezeway."

Sitting in the shade, watching cars blur by on Charleston, I wondered if the cabby who dropped me off would pick me up. It was a long shot, I realized, but the thought made me smile. I could tell him I talked to several senior citizens, including Steve and Betty, and I understand what he meant when he said, "Don't think that your little fears are big ones." It was good advice for someone checking into the Blue Angel. There was nothing to be afraid of—except your preconceptions. The only ghosts were personal demons. The enemy lurked in the mirror or window (not in the closet or room next door) and gripped a syringe or glass pipe (not a knife or gun).

Last night in this same spot, Steve mentioned Louis L'Amour. In L'Amour's Old West, drifters rode into town on horses, drank and gambled in swinging-door saloons, and slept under the stars. In the New West, they arrive on Greyhounds, drink and gamble in Western-themed casinos, and sleep at the Blue Angel.

A taxi turned into the driveway, pulling me from my thoughts. I stood and waved. It sped into the breezeway and squeaked to a stop, then its doors unlocked. I followed my bags into the back seat.

"The Diplomat apartments," I said, looking at the cabby in the rearview mirror. He was wearing a baseball cap and shades and had a bushy gray mustache. "Paradise and Sierra Vista, just south of DI."

"OK," he said, shifting into drive.

"How's it going?"

"Not too bad. Just came out." His voice was as gravelly as the pool.

"Starting your day at the Blue Angel, huh? Come here often?"

"Actually, I used to live here."

I leaned forward. "You serious?"

"Yep. When I first got to town. I stayed on the second floor." He pointed toward the angel, as she watched us drive away.

"When was that?"

"Nineteen ninety-one."

"What was it like then?"

"Same as it is now," he said, turning right on Fremont. "Pretty shabby."

"I stayed there a week," I said, looking back at the arches. "I'm a writer and I was curious about the place."

"What was it like?"

"Not bad. It's cheap and bare-bones, but it's safe and clean. The managers do the best they can with it. What'd you think?"

"Well, that was a long time ago and I only stayed a few months." He turned on Eastern.

"I only stayed seven days, but it felt like seven weeks. It dragged out. The people are nice, just down-and-out. I got hit up a lot for money and food and cigarettes."

"Yeah, it's a blighted neighborhood."

"Was it any better when you stayed there?"

"About the same. But I went and got a job as soon as I could. I can't stand begging for money and bumming cigarettes and stuff like that. I was driving a taxi within a couple months."

"And you been doing it ever since?"

"Nah. I went and drove a truck for thirteen years."

As we cruised south on Eastern, the two-way radio crackled and the dispatcher sent a cab to the Western. "When the dispatcher sent you to the Blue Angel, what were your thoughts?"

"I just remembered that you could get to it from Charleston, even though it has a Fremont Street address. I hadn't been there in a while, but I remembered the shortcut."

"You have any specific memories of the place?"

He paused, then flashed a smoker's smile. "Yeah."

"But none you can share with me? Good ones or bad ones?"

"Good ones, I suppose. I was so poor when I got here. I had three hundred dollars in my pocket and the room was seventy-five dollars a week. I was just trying to survive, but the future was bright. I had high hopes." He turned on DI. "One thing I do remember is they spelled the 'Office' sign with three Fs. That kind of confused me."

I looked at him in the mirror and laughed. "I guess they fixed that typo. I would've noticed that."

Late afternoon Wednesday, after I interviewed Steve and before Game Five of the Lakers-Nuggets series, the power went out at the Blue Angel. Tenants stared out the windows, stood in the door frames, and leaned on the balcony railings: gray-haired men with artistic mustaches; plain-faced middle-aged women; acne-faced boys in baseball caps turned backward. The gaunt, sandpaper-skinned cabby wouldn't have looked out of place among them. I could see him leaning on the railing, smoking a cigarette, exhaling all his worries and watching them drift away in the wind.

"You miss the Blue Angel?" I said.

"I miss the rent. It's a hundred and fifty dollars a week now?"

"Yeah. A hundred and thirty, plus a twenty-dollar deposit."

"They have any monthly deals?"

"No. They only do weekly. Why? What's going on?"

"I'm thinking about moving back in. I'm not doing too hot right now and I'm spending two hundred dollars a week on rent."

"Where you staying?"

"The Siegel Suites on Tropicana. It's only a few blocks from work. It's convenient." He turned left on Swenson Street, then right on Sierra Vista.

"You'd move back to the Blue Angel?"

"If I had to. If things got real bad, and they're pretty bad now. I can't afford to pay two hundred a week with the money I'm making. The recession has hurt this town bad. If there's not a convention, there's no money to be made."

"What are your options?"

"I don't know. I was thinking about trucking again or trying to get a job with my computer skills. I'm making five hundred dollars every two weeks, plus tips. It's depressing. And the thought of having to move to a place like the Blue Angel is really getting me down."

At the end of a row of low-slung stucco buildings, the Diplomat appeared on the south side of the street.

"Just pull up to the side of the building," I said, pointing toward the dumpsters.

The cabby cut on his blinker and angled into the parking lot. "I mean, you get used to it after a while. It begins to dim whatever hope you have of the future, of getting out of there, and it starts to look better. It starts to feel like home, but I don't want to fool myself like that again."

"I don't either," I said, squinting at the meter. I handed him $25, reached for the bags, then opened the door.

Doaud Allison

OUT ON PAROLE

A SWIRL OF STEEL, PLEXIGLAS, AND BARBWIRE, the Southern Desert Correctional Center sparkles like a mirage on the edge of Indian Springs. High Desert State Prison sprawls to the west. Cars blur by on U.S. Highway 95. Otherwise, the terrain is bleak and barren—cow skulls, creosote, and miles and miles of sand.

Southern Desert is the antithesis of Alcatraz, surrounded and secured by a *lack* of water.

On March 31, 2005, as the sun began its merciful descent, Doaud Allison (also known as David Allison) entered an office in unit one of the prison. Allison matched the details of his inmate record: five-foot-nine, 220 pounds, dark complexion. His head was shaved and shiny. Muscles bulged from his body like mountains from the desert floor. He wore a collared shirt, blue jeans, and sneakers. A knit cap hung from his back pocket.

Allison, 28, sat in a chair and set his hands on his knees. His brown eyes, slightly crossed, darted about the office. Dana Serrata, a parole coordinator with the Nevada Department of Corrections, pushed a stack of paper across her desk. Allison picked it up and flipped through it, stroking his beard.

"Make sure you register as a felon and don't forget to get your Social Security card," said Serrata.

Allison nodded, then set the stack of paper on the edge of the desk and rubbed his thighs.

"There are so many things going through my mind," he said. "Right now, it's tough to stop and focus on one thought. I'm not second-guessing myself, but you look at the recidivism rate and you got to wonder."

Nationally, about 70% of parolees return to prison.

Since convicted of murder in 1993, Allison has been held in four prisons: Southern Desert, the Southern Nevada Correctional Center, Nevada State Prison, and the Northern Nevada Correctional Center. He got a GED and credits from Northern Nevada Community College. He also participated in the Going Home Prepared program, which offers classes (Victim Empathy, Relapse Prevention, Criminal Thinking Errors) and counseling to violent convicts who'll be 14 to 35 years old when released.

"David was presented to the parole board with no institutional violence, no escape history, only one disciplinary for a minor offense, and a record of working or going to school the entire time he's been incarcerated," said Serrata. "His positive programming and work record likely had much to do with the board's decision to release him."

Allison rocked in the chair, head down. The sound of his hands rubbing denim was drowned out by inmates in the hallway. He lifted his head and cracked a smile.

"I know the world has changed a lot, but I'm looking forward to it," said Allison. "It's a strange feeling. I'm nervous. I wasn't nervous yesterday, but I am today. I'm ready, though.

"It'll be a piece of cake."

ON APRIL 26, 1992, when he was 15 years old, Allison killed 19-year-old Francisco Dominguez during a carjacking.

According to the police report, Allison and three young men were cruising the streets of North Las Vegas in a Chevrolet Monte Carlo, looking for a score. They targeted a house on Spear Street, but someone was home, so they continued to cruise. Soon they spotted a 1986 Oldsmobile with shiny rims parked on Evans Avenue. A group of young men were leaning on the Olds.

Carrying a pistol, Allison climbed out of the Monte Carlo and demanded the keys to the car. Three of the young men ran; Francisco Dominguez and his brother Fernando stood still. Allison shot Francisco Dominguez and again demanded the keys. Dominguez dropped them on the ground. Allison froze.

"I thought the gun was on safety," he said. "I wasn't trying to kill anyone. I just wanted to scare him."

One of the accomplices jumped out of the Monte Carlo and picked up the keys. When he opened the Oldsmobile's driver-side door, an alarm went off. He and Allison jumped back in the Chevy. It sped west on Evans, disappearing into the darkness.

An ambulance arrived and took Dominguez to University Medical Center, where he died a few hours later.

The next day, North Las Vegas Police Department detectives tracked down Allison at his grandmother's house and brought him in for questioning. Allison admitted he shot Dominguez and took full responsibility for the crime.

He was charged with first-degree murder, attempted robbery, and other related offenses. In March 1993, he was convicted and sentenced to life in prison with the possibility of parole.

"I was happy with the sentence," said Allison, whose juvenile record included battery and carrying a concealed weapon. "I knew I had a chance to get back into society. But I was devastated, too. It was hard.

"Looking back, I wonder why I did it and why I was there. It really hurt me that I took someone's life. I'm really remorseful about the pain I caused his family and my family. If I could, I'd take it all away."

News of Allison's release devastated the Dominguez family. Ana Fletcher, Francisco Dominguez's sister, said the family wasn't contacted by the parole board. They didn't know Allison was going to be released.

"We were really surprised," said Fletcher. "We assumed he wasn't going to be up for parole until he served at least fifteen years and that someone was going to contact us. That's all we knew."

Fernando Dominguez recalled the crime, which he said has haunted him.

"My hands went up," said Dominguez. "He [Allison] pointed the gun at me and said, 'Give me the keys!' I said I didn't have the keys. He came closer to me and pointed the gun at my head. Then he took the gun off me and pointed it at my brother. My brother got scared. He started walking backwards and the guy shot him."

Francisco Dominguez was the youngest of 11 children. News of the release was particularly hard on his mother, said Fletcher.

"We want to know why we were never contacted," she said. "We wanted to at least go to the parole hearings and have some say in this."

David Smith, a spokesman for the parole board, said victims or their families have to submit a written request to be notified of hearings. If a request isn't on file, victims or their families aren't contacted.

"It's a very sensitive issue," said Smith, noting the Dominguez family didn't submit a request. "Some victims don't want to be notified. They don't want to be reminded of the crime every time someone has a parole hearing. So does notification become a passive or active activity? Do we notify them even if they don't want to be notified? We have to assume, if they haven't requested it, they don't want to be notified at all."

Smith delivered more bad news to the Dominguez family. Frank Blocks, one of Allison's accomplices, was paroled in October 2003.

"This has been very, very traumatic," said Fletcher. "We've had to tell our brothers about all this. We've been trying to calm them down. Of course, they want revenge, but the family doesn't want that. We want to try to find out more about what happened and why we weren't contacted. Hopefully, we'll get the answers and go from there. We want to put this behind us."

AT NINE-THIRTY A.M. ON APRIL 1, a van pulled up in front of the Division of Parole and Probation building near Rancho Drive and Bonanza Road. The driver jumped out and opened the side door. A line of ex-cons filed out, carrying plastic bags and cardboard boxes. Dressed in his "prison blues," Allison stood in the parking lot and looked up. The sky was perfect blue, horizon to horizon. A breeze swept across the asphalt, rustling the trees bordering the lot. Birds chirped.

Allison exhaled. For the first time in 13 years, he was free.

"It hit me when I stepped out of the van and no one told me to go inside the building," he said. "It was like, 'You have a choice to go in or you can leave. It's up to you.' I had the chance to make my own decision. I could do what I wanted to.

"Also, I heard a bird chirp. The birds in prison, they don't chirp or nothing; it's crazy. But when we pulled up and I stood outside, they were chirping. That's when I knew I was free."

Allison and his girlfriend Aja (pronounced Asia), who arrived after the van, entered the building and were escorted into the office of social worker Sharon Williams. Williams opened a folder and handed Allison a copy of his birth certificate. While flipping through a stack of paper, she reminded him to register as an ex-felon.

"About fifty percent of ex-offenders are going to follow their parole plan almost to the letter," said Williams, a social worker since 1989. "Twenty-five percent are going to need a push, a reminder. They come out of prison thinking they can do this without any help. The last twenty-five percent already have an agenda. Regardless of what we say or do, they are not going to do what they're supposed to."

Throughout the meeting, which focused on job opportunities and people he could call if he had questions, Allison nodded attentively. Finally, Williams handed him a day planner, a bus schedule, and 10 bus tokens.

"The Going Home Prepared program has about a seventy percent success ratio," said social worker Jim Henson, who has worked in corrections for 30 years. "Compared to the normal recidivism rate of the Department of Corrections, it's the opposite; they're having about a seventy percent failure rate. Going Home Prepared's success is primarily due to the intense supervision, the services we're providing for the individuals before they get out, and knocking down some of the basic barriers."

Barriers include getting a photo ID, Social Security card, housing, and a job.

"They're released with twenty-five dollars—and that's it," said Henson. "They have twenty-five dollars and we're telling them, 'OK, now go out there and be successful!' They have no identification, no way to cash that check, and no job leads."

There are 11,000 prisoners in the Nevada Department of Corrections. Two thousand to 3,000 of them qualify for the Going Home Prepared program, said Serrata. Currently, 220 people are in the program.

Luckily for him, Allison is one of them. But that didn't seem to comfort him as he left the Division of Parole and Probation, clutching a folder full of paper, and walked toward Aja's car.

"I have butterflies in my stomach, because I don't really know what to expect," said Allison. "There are so many things going through my mind. I've always dreamed of this moment, but now it's time to make the dream come true."

Allison left most of his possessions (clothes, toiletries, electronics) at Southern Desert. He didn't want physical reminders of his time in prison, he said, and the inmates would need them more than he would. All he had was a $200 check (money his family mailed him while he was in prison), the "blues" on his back, and the bus tokens.

"Even before I made parole, years and years ago, I thought about this moment," he said. "How do I feel? I feel good, but I also know that I got to succeed, because there are so many people counting on me.

"When one person leaves a prison, a lot of people leave with them. You've been there so long and you got relationships and you get close to people. They see you off and everybody's saying goodbye. But there's a hurtful side to it, too, because there are certain guys who are never going home.

"So I'm doing this for myself, but also for them."

A WEEK LATER, ALLISON RETURNED to the Division of Parole and Probation dressed in a polo shirt, baggy jeans, and sneakers. (He'd thrown away his "prison blues.") He was also wearing glasses. Sitting in the lobby, clutching the folder full of paper, he leaned back and exhaled.

Allison's first week on the outside was fairly mundane. He hung out with family and friends. He shopped for clothes, spending his savings. And he tried and failed to get a Social Security card and picture ID. (The Department of Corrections had the wrong Social Security number on file and is searching for the right one.)

"It's been mixed," said Allison. "It's been up and down. There are things I want to do that I can't because I don't have an ID. There are places I want to go that I can't because I don't have a car; I got to have someone drive me around. All that tears at me a little bit, but I'm also overwhelmed and overjoyed about getting my life going again."

A receptionist emerged from a Plexiglas office and pointed Allison to a shelf, where he found a parole and probation monthly report. Its front side included questions about community service, restitution, and supervision fees. A budget grid covered the back side.

Allison began to fill out the report.

Ronald Satterwhite, Allison's parole officer, entered the lobby. He escorted Allison to a hallway, put on latex gloves, and handed him a paper cup. He then followed him into a restroom.

After collecting a urine sample, Satterwhite escorted Allison to his office. They sat and Satterwhite began flipping through a parole agreement, still wearing the gloves. He went over it requirement by requirement: report to your parole officer once a month; keep your parole officer updated on where you live and who you live with; no alcohol or drugs; no weapons; be careful of whom you associate with.

"Otherwise, you're pretty much on your own," said Satterwhite, who supervises 35 parolees. "No curfew. You can pretty much do what you want. There's not going to be anybody looking over your shoulder."

Satterwhite told Allison he has to pay a $30-a-month parole supervision fee and $20 a month in restitution. The parole agreement is for life, he said.

"Do you have any questions?" said Satterwhite.

"Nah," said Allison.

Satterwhite and Allison signed the agreement. Then Satterwhite handed Allison a tongue depressor to insert in his mouth, collecting a DNA sample. Finally, Allison left his thumbprints on a sheet of paper.

"Generally speaking, most of the ex-offenders in the Going Home Prepared program are young men who have spent the last five or six years in prison," said Satterwhite, who estimates that 20% of his parolees break the agreement and return to prison. "They went in as young men and they didn't have driver's licenses. They didn't finish high school. They've never been employed. It's a concern with just about all of them: Are they going to be able to readjust? Are they going to be able to find a job and get on the straight and narrow?"

In the parking lot, Allison reflected on his first week out of prison. He said he has struggled to adjust to new technology, particularly computers and cell phones. "Things are different—way different—from thirteen years ago," he said. "It's like you need a degree to use some of this stuff."

He has also had trouble removing the "mask" he wore in prison and leaving that mentality behind.

"Out here, people use the words 'punk' and 'bitch' fluently," said Allison, who moved in with his cousin and her family in southeast Las Vegas. "In prison, those words can cost you your life. When I'm around people who use that kind of language, I have to remind myself that I'm not on the inside anymore.

"One of my family members used one of those words. I was ready to react, but I caught myself. I was like, 'OK, I got to sit him down and talk to him and let him know we don't talk like that where I come from.' I had to let him know my state of mind. I'm easing down on it, but I ain't going to let no one disrespect me."

The sun glared at Allison like a judge from the bench. Heat waves rose from the asphalt, foreshadowing summer and blurring the landscape. Allison looked across the parking lot—no barbwire fence, razor-ribbon coils, or guard towers. Aja's car idled nearby.

"I'm nervous," said Allison. "But at the same time, I'm optimistic. I'm trying to keep a positive attitude. I'm preparing myself for next week, when I have all my identification and when it's time for me to start looking for a job. I'm anxious, very anxious. But I'm also scared, because there's a lot of things out here I don't know about."

ON MAY 18, MORE THAN A MONTH AND A HALF after his release, Allison was hunched over a table at Republic Services trash company. His wallet lay open, next to a cell phone he was still learning to use. Business cards, a Social Security card, and a picture ID were strewn about the tabletop.

Allison's left hand stroked his chin. His right hand held a pen, which moved tentatively across a job application: name, address, Social Security number, position, salary expected. And then, of course, *the* question: Have you ever been convicted of a crime?

"I thought, 'Here we go again,'" said Allison. "Yeah, I did what I did. I can't change that. But I served my time. I spent half my life in prison. Now I'm trying to start over and this question keeps coming back to haunt me."

One of 2,500 parolees released into Las Vegas each year, Allison spent his second week out of prison trying to get his Social Security card and a picture ID. It proved to be an adventure.

When Allison was 10, his father was murdered in front of him in a Brooklyn, New York, apartment. His drug-addict mother had disappeared and Allison, in possession of his dad's Social Security card, moved to Las Vegas to live with an aunt. When arrested, he entered the Department of Corrections under his dad's name (David) and Social Security number.

"In order for us to get him a driver's license, we had to have his Social Security card," said parole coordinator Serrata. "Well, we couldn't get his Social Security card because we didn't have the right number. Finally, we were able to determine what his real Social Security number was, and they were able to issue him a replacement card, but it took a lot of digging and research to figure it out."

After getting his Social Security card, Allison scoured the valley for work. He visited JobConnect (a statewide network of businesses and prospective workers) and a handful of temp agencies. He also applied at construction companies.

"Trying to find work has been the biggest challenge," said Allison. "It doesn't seem like anyone wants to deal with me because I've been in prison. It seems like doors are getting slammed in my face left and right."

At one temp agency, Allison filled out the application (admitting he'd been convicted of a felony) and handed it to a staffer. The staffer looked it over, paused, and asked about the conviction. Allison explained the crime and sentence.

The company doesn't hire convicted murderers, said the staffer.

"Once I tell them 'murder,' I look at their expression and I can tell that they're shocked," said Allison. "But as I converse with them, I ease them down—especially when they find out I was fifteen years old when I committed the crime and I served my time. But a lot of this is about policy. A lot of companies just don't deal with that kind of stuff.

"They try to put you down easy, but it hurts. It hurts because I feel that I've done my time, but I'm still being punished and I'm still being judged. I had to prove to the parole board that I've changed and now I have to prove it to other people in society. It seems like I'm always trying to prove myself."

Allison continued to fill out the Republic Services application: age, job history, professional skills, education, references. Finally, the pen stopped and he leaned back in the chair.

A few minutes later, Human Resources Assistant Hope Graham approached the table and sat across from Allison. Graham flipped through the application, credentials swinging from her neck, and scribbled in the margins.

"Computer skills?" she asked, beginning Allison's first job interview since being released.

"A little bit, but not a whole lot," he said.

"Can you type?"

"A little bit, but not a lot."

"A little pecking?"

"Yeah, a little bit."

"I'll put down 'light'—not that typing has anything to do with picking up garbage," said Graham.

Allison laughed.

"You used to physical work?" Graham continued.

"Oh yeah," said Allison. "That's *no* problem."

Graham said Republic Services couldn't guarantee full-time work, but part-time work was available. "Pitchers" (non-drivers who throw trash into the trucks) start at $17.60 an hour, she said.

"We treat ex-felons on a case-by-case basis," said Human Resources Director Romeo Vellutini, who wandered in and out of the interview room. "We have a pretty good record of hiring ex-felons, and we always have. Our major concern is violent felons, people with assaults and things of that nature."

Graham told Allison he had to take a psychological exam and drug test. He'd also be subjected to a background check, she said.

"If everything goes well, orientation is held every Friday," said Graham.

Allison smiled and nodded. "OK. Sounds good."

"You ready?" she asked him, standing up.

"Yes, ma'am."

Graham escorted Allison to a cubicle, where she set up the exam. Thirty minutes later, clutching pre-employment forms, Allison exited the building and strutted toward the parking lot.

"I'm very optimistic," he said. "I'm just hoping I can get this job. It's a good opportunity for me and it would help me provide for myself. Actually, I'm happy about just being able to get an interview. At least I finally got through the door and was able to talk to somebody."

Two weeks after the interview, Allison received a form letter from Republic Services. It said he didn't get the job.

"When I got the letter, it kind of messed me up," said Allison. "I was like, 'Damn, why did I go to the interview and take a urinalysis and a physical?' That right there got my hopes up—not only my hopes, but also my family's hopes. Everyone I talked to felt like I had the job, then I get the letter saying that they're going with someone else.

"It was discouraging. I felt down for a minute, but I know that depression is not an ally. I don't want to do nothing stupid that will put me back in prison. I just got to find other avenues."

Vellutini explained, "What happened this year is that we haven't really experienced the surge in employment that we usually experience when it gets hot. It hasn't really been that hot lately and we haven't hired as many people as we have in past years. The other factor is that Mr. Allison applied for a pitcher job, and that's probably the number-one job applied for because it's not necessarily a skilled position."

Vellutini said Republic Services has 500 pitcher applications on file. Allison's is among them, he said, and he's a candidate for future positions.

SUMMER SETTLED IN. The sun burned like a neon sign and suffocating breezes swept down the streets, which were empty—except for air-conditioned cars and shirtless madmen predicting the Second Coming. Dust reigned. Shade was scarce. Seemingly melting, the hotel-casinos shimmered in the heat.

Taking refuge, Doaud Allison sat on a couch in his cousin's house, a drum machine balanced on his lap. He banged away at the buttons, like a video poker fiend, and tweaked the knobs. A heavy bassline eased from the speakers.

"As you can tell, that's kind of dark and gloomy," said Allison. "At the time I made that, I was feeling pretty down. See, I think music is just another form of expression. I also got beats from when I was feeling happy, when I wasn't so dark and melancholic.

"I can just come back here and put something down," he continued, explaining that the drum machine serves as an escape. "I just go for what I know. Sometimes I don't even make music. I just sit here and toy with it. It helps take my mind off things."

Indeed, Allison has had a lot to think about over the past three months. He struggled to adjust to new technology. He had trouble getting his Social Security card and a picture ID. He had to relearn the etiquette of everyday life. He had to pay parole supervision fees and restitution. He couldn't find a job.

"The prison system is just a warehouse," said Allison. "You can go to school and things like that, but the classes don't prepare you for what you go through out here in society. They don't prepare you for anything. It's on you. You have to do everything yourself."

During his job search, Allison reflected on his time in prison: He read self-help and spiritual books, played chess and lifted weights, and worked in the license-plate plant. But he didn't learn a trade.

"If the prison system had better vocational training, it would've been a whole lot different for me," he said. "I could've had a lot of work, but I don't have any welding experience. In prison, they have welding classes. But every time you try to enroll in them, they're full or they get canceled. There isn't much available."

Allison said the Department of Corrections also needs more computer classes.

Serrata admitted the department isn't perfect, but said it has improved. "I think we're finally on the way to developing a successful coordinated re-entry program with Going Home Prepared as the template. The director of the Department of Corrections, Jackie Crawford, acknowledged prior to GHP that the re-entry method in Nevada didn't work and did little to prevent recidivism. We've set a precedent in Nevada for organizing and coordinating services and referrals among a variety of agencies, which makes a difference."

Serrata said the department doesn't have the resources to train inmates for work, but it encourages them to work (paid or unpaid) in the prison system and get a high-school diploma or GED. It also encourages them to take college classes.

"Data shows that there's a direct link to post-release success and education," said Howard Skolnik, spokesman for the Department of Corrections. "A functionally illiterate inmate has less than a thirty-three-percent chance of success after release. A college graduate only has a six percent likelihood of returning to prison after release.

"We're proud that the educational programming offered to our inmates is equivalent to that offered in the community and that the education an inmate receives prepares him every bit as much for success as the education provided in the community."

Allison turned down the music. Setting the drum machine on the couch and cracking a smile, he said he got a job loading and unloading trucks at Walker Furniture for nine dollars an hour.

"When I got the job, I was like: 'Finally!'" said Allison, who found the job through a friend and ex-con. "It took a lot longer than I thought it would. In prison, I was thinking it wouldn't take that long. In prison, I thought everything would just happen on the spot.

"I'm happy now. I'm working at Walker Furniture and a temp agency. I'm building up my résumé. It doesn't pay much, but it's an inspiration because I'm not stagnant anymore. I feel like I'm mobile. I feel like I'm moving toward something better for myself."

Eventually, Allison wants a higher-paying job. He also wants an apprenticeship with the Ironworkers Union, which accepted him into its training program, and to be a personal trainer.

Then he wants to buy a car and move out of his cousin's house.

"Yeah, I want to get my own place," he said, smile broadening.

With those words, Allison picked up the drum machine and placed it on his lap. He banged the buttons and tweaked the knobs. Jazzy cymbals, angelic synthesizers, and a light bassline shot from the speakers.

"This is something I made when I was feeling a bit cooler," said Allison. "Really, my feelings are up and down. I'm proud of myself because by now some people probably would've been back in prison. I'm proud that I'm still out here handling my business. But I'm mad because I feel like society—and I know I committed a hell of a crime—has given me another sentence. I feel like I'm being penalized twice.

"But I'm going to be all right," he said, nodding to the beat. "I know I'm going to be all right. I'm going to make it happen for myself. It just takes a little time."

DEATH OF THE DOUBLE-WIDE

IF YOU WANT A SCARE ON HALLOWEEN, don't explore an abandoned hotel-casino. Don't walk the back alleys of Fremont Street. Don't read Edgar Allan Poe stories in a storm drain.

Simply take a stroll through the Tropicana Mobile Home Park at midnight. Your chest will tighten. Your stomach will go hollow. Chills will shoot down your spine and shake your soul.

See, the Tropicana Mobile Home Park is in the process of closing. The land was sold to a developer in May. Tenants were told to move out by the end of November. Some of them have moved out; some remain.

So what you have is a trailer park that isn't open or closed, functioning or entirely dysfunctional, alive or dead.

Shells of old trailers sit on lots, entrails spilling out of open doors and windows. Household appliances are strewn across lawns. But don't bother complaining to management. The office is deserted, like a command post in a lost war. The pool has been drained. Stray cats—many of them black—dash across the streets, rib cages showing.

The abandoned trailers have been looted, said tenants. Awnings and steps have been stripped and scrapped for money. Street people have moved in.

"It's dangerous in here," said Jane Robertson, who has lived at the park for 11 years. "Every little noise I hear, I'm up. It's a damn shame what's happened to this place."

Robertson said when she leaves her trailer, she turns on the TV to keep looters away. And she's not impressed with the security guards who patrol the park at night.

They're there to protect the land, she said, not the tenants.

"It's getting very scary," said Robertson's neighbor Annmarie Gibson. "It's spooky. Most of the trailers are empty. They finally got some security in here from six p.m. to six a.m., but that's just within the last week or so. We have one homeless lady who's so comfortable living here she said hello to me in the laundry room the other day.

"I've seen people in here who I've never seen before," continued Gibson, holding her three-year-old son Liam. "There are people in here all the time who don't belong here. The other morning there was a pickup truck in front of one of the trailers. The lady who lived there had been gone for a month and a half. They were just loading stuff up. They drove out of here with a truck full of stuff."

Sadly, this horror show is not unique to the Tropicana Mobile Home Park. It's being played at trailer parks throughout Las Vegas, which are closing at a frightening rate—leaving behind broken bonds, promises, and dreams.

IT STARTS WITH A RUMOR. The rumor spreads on porches, over chain-link fences, and at mailboxes, grocery stores, video-poker bars, and American Legion posts. A month or two later, a notice is posted on the trailer doors:

"This letter is to inform you that Such & Such Mobile Home Park is under new ownership. We are pleased to announce that our current management team will remain in place and will continue to be responsible for all management duties, including collecting rent and enforcing park rules. They will also continue to be responsible for park maintenance. If you have any questions or concerns regarding the park, please call the office."

The notice confuses tenants new to the trailer-park lifestyle. Some disregard it. Some call the office and ask questions: Who are the new

owners? What are they like? What are their plans for the park? Some actually think things may be better under the new owners.

Veterans of the lifestyle, however, know what comes next. Another notice, a few days later: "Pursuant to state law, you are hereby notified that Such & Such Mobile Home Park will be closed and you have 180 days to vacate. If you do not vacate by that time, you will be in violation of state law and the appropriate action will be taken. Please schedule a meeting with the manager to discuss your options."

The tenants smile sarcastically and shake their heads. They share the notice with their roommates (friends, co-workers, brothers, daughters, mothers, and grandmothers). Some remain calm. Some freak out. Some simply cry.

At least that's how it happened at La Jolla Mobile Home Park.

"It's utter bullshit," said tenant John Giordano, who has lived at the park for nine years. "First we get a notice saying the park has been sold, but nothing's changing. Then three days later, they tell us we have six months to get out. You'd at least think they'd say, 'Hey, we have a prospective buyer and we'd like to get your feelings about it.' At least give the people who live here the first shot at buying the park. A lot of us would've gone to the bank and tried to buy the land we're living on. Hell, we would've jumped at the opportunity."

Patrice Adams, 78, lives one street up from Giordano. Adams paid $54,000 for her double-wide, which has been anchored at the park for more than 12 years. Her rent is $350 a month. She lives off Social Security, struggling to get by since her husband died of heart failure a few years ago.

Adams shares the trailer with her daughter, two granddaughters, great grandson, and four dogs.

By law, La Jolla's new owner has to pay to move the trailer up to 50 miles. If Adams decides not to move the trailer or if it can't be moved, the owner pays "fair market value" for the trailer—minus the cost of removal and disposal.

If Adams decides to move the trailer, it will take two to four weeks to disassemble, transport, and reassemble. During that time, she'll have to pay for housing, storage, food, and other expenses.

Angelique Adams

"I don't really mind moving," said Adams, "but I'm going to have to find storage for my furniture for at least 14 days. We have to move into a motel. Then there's all the food we have to buy because we'll have to go out to eat. We've got to pay for kennels.

"Everyone helps out, but we barely make ends meet as it is."

La Jolla's manager gave tenants a list of trailer parks in the area with comparable rents. But most of the parks are full and some are closing, said Patrice's granddaughter Angelique Adams.

Also, she said, 180 days is not enough notice.

"Six months doesn't even begin to give anybody a chance to start saving money," said Angelique Adams. "A lot of people here are old and on fixed incomes. It doesn't give them a chance to get anything together, especially with the holidays coming up. These expenses are, like, three times what Christmas would've cost."

Added Patrice Adams, referring to Angelique's nine-year-old son Patrick, "We've got a little boy here. You can't tell him he's not going to have Christmas. He won't understand that."

After being offered $12,000 for the trailer, the Adams family decided to move it to Casa Linda Mobile Home Park on East Lake Mead Boulevard. Their rent will be $100 more a month than at La Jolla.

"Houses are too expensive here and they're built so crappy anyway," said Angelique Adams. "We couldn't live in a condo, because we have dogs. Plus, they're so small and expensive. We really had no other option.

"Even though it's a mobile home, it's still a place to live. It beats being on the streets."

WHAT CAN TENANTS DO WHEN the notice is posted on the doors? When they have three kids and two jobs? When they're 75 years old? When they're handicapped? When they're living Social Security check to Social Security check?

The short answer is very little.

Though called "mobile homes," most of the trailers are no more mobile than a suburban tract house. They're big (porches, car ports, and other add-ons). They're old. They're structurally weak. They don't have undercarriages. They're rooted to their foundations with braces, electric wires, and utility pipes.

Even if the homes were mobile, there are few places in Las Vegas to move them. Fourteen trailer parks have closed or will close in Clark County in 2005, more than the previous seven years combined. (The last park to open was Sunrise Gardens in 2000.) Many of the remaining 135 or so parks are full or have strict regulations: no pets, no double-wides, no trailers more than 10 years old, no tenants under the age of 55. And with the high demand for lots—more than 1,450 spaces will be lost this year—rents have gone up.

Consequently, many tenants are forced to sell their trailers to the owner.

"I get them calling me on Monday morning," said Allen Scott, an investigator with the Nevada Division of Manufactured Housing. "'Maybe I ought to kill myself,' they say. 'I'm too old to deal with this.' What can you tell someone who's feeling that way? I just tell them it's not as bad as they think and not to panic."

After selling their trailers and getting back, say, $10,000 from a $50,000 investment, tenants have to find a place to live. This can be a challenge. Homes in Las Vegas are usually not an option, as they average about $300,000. The average price of a condo is $200,000. Apartments are an option, but they're typically at least $400 more a month than trailer parks.

That leaves weekly motels and the streets as the only options for some tenants.

"I'm going to be out on the streets pushing around a cart," said Shirley Baker, who lives at and manages Diamond Head Trailer Park. "Doesn't Las Vegas have enough homeless people already? That's where I'm going to be, with a sign that says 'Will Work for Food.' That's where we're all going to be."

Diamond Head, which is located on East Fremont Street, was sold in August 2004. It's scheduled to close in the spring.

Its tenants are mostly senior citizens and working-class families, said Baker. Rent is about $300 a month.

"I'm getting the hell out of Las Vegas; this town doesn't like me," said tenant Sam Dalton, who plans to move to Elko, Nevada. "I have property on the north end of the state, but what about these people? They've got kids. They don't have much money. There's nothing they can do but go homeless—along with their kids."

Added T.J. Fournier, who has lived at the park for four years, "When I moved in, I told the manager I wasn't going to live anywhere else. I thought I was going to die here."

Diamond Head's old and new owners did not return phone calls. But Marolyn Mann, executive director of Manufactured Home Community Owners, a nonprofit organization that represents the owners and managers, defended the owners and state law.

Mann, the organization's executive director since 1986, said most trailer parks in Las Vegas are owned by families, not corporations. The families are in business to make money, she said, but also because they like the lifestyle and tenants. They're not getting rich off $350-a-month rents.

Recently, Mann continued, the city of Las Vegas and Clark County have "cracked down" on trailer parks. She blamed the crackdown on Sky Vue Mobile Home Park, which was closed by the city in April 2004 because of health and safety violations. Since then, she said, owners have been forced to bring parks up to code at their own expense.

At the same time as the crackdown, said Mann, land prices in Las Vegas were soaring. Suddenly, developers and investment companies were offering the families millions of dollars for their aging trailer parks.

"They've told me it's just time," said Mann of the families. "They've owned these parks for a long time and they just can't afford to meet current codes. It makes sense for them to sell."

But what about the tenants?

"They're treated fairly," said Mann. "We realize they're in a unique situation, but protections are in place. As far as I know, we're the only industry that helps move tenants when they have to relocate. There's compensation and there are places for them to move. They're taken care of."

Nonetheless, tenants remain defiant and state workers sympathetic.

"It's a sad business," said Renee Diamond, administrator of the Nevada Division of Manufactured Housing. "It isn't just senior citizens who are affected. There are families, too. A lot of these people can't afford the down payment or the price of a new home, so they don't have anywhere to go. Sooner or later, it's going to impact the service-industry workers on the Strip.

"If they can't afford to live here, how are they going to work here?"

THIS IS WHERE WE'RE SUPPOSED TO TELL YOU that the city and county are giving tax breaks to developers who build affordable housing. That a state senator or assembly member is sponsoring a bill to save the trailer parks. That the hotel-casinos are building affordable housing for their workers.

But in fact, there's little collaboration between the government

County Commissioner Tom Collins

and developers. No politician is sponsoring a bill to save the parks. And the casinos seem to have more pressing concerns than housing— like trying to come up with clever new ways to separate you from your money.

When it learned of the park closings, the county explored its options. It considered moving tenants to other parks ... before realizing they were closing, too. It checked to see if any new parks were opening: Developers are going vertical, the county soon realized, not horizontal. And it consulted the Bureau of Land Management about land in the rurals, but discovered nothing was available.

Finally, the county settled on trying to help tenants who remain at the parks after they close.

"We don't know what can be done at the government level," said Assistant County Manager Darryl Martin. "We think the focus has to be on building more housing; the focus has to be on the development side. All we can do is figure out ways to provide subsidies, whether they're land or tax breaks, to encourage developers to build afford-able housing. That's what we need to do."

County Commissioner Tom Collins, who grew up in trailer parks, echoed Martin.

"The government needs to figure out a way to provide more spaces," said Collins, a Democrat. "Federal law allows us to go get BLM land and to get a park built on it. We need to encourage devel-opers to go out and acquire this land and build mobile-home parks on it. That's what I'm trying to do in my district."

But there *are* barriers, said Collins. There's little coordination between federal, state, and local government, he said, and the Bush administration isn't concerned about trailer-park closings.

"The Republicans don't give a damn about anybody who ain't got a pile of money," said Collins.

So there you have it: The city and county are forcing owners to bring trailer parks up to code at their own expense. Land prices are soaring. Developers and investment companies are offering the own-ers millions of dollars for the parks. It makes sense for them to sell, said Mann.

By law, tenants have 180 days to vacate the parks. The owners will pay to move trailers up to 50 miles. Of course, the trailers take two to four weeks to disassemble, transport, and reassemble. During that time, tenants have to pay for housing, storage, food, and other expenses.

If the trailers can't be moved, the owners pay "fair market value" for them—minus the cost of removal and disposal. Tenants get back one-fifth of what they paid for the trailers. Then they have to find a place to live ... a place they can afford, a place that will accept their pets and grandchildren, a place that will embrace their quirks. A place that doesn't exist in Las Vegas.

Government workers and politicians have no answers. What can we do, they say? A man has a right to sell his property. It's free enter-prise. It's evidence the system is working.

So it's up to Big Business—developers, investment companies, the gambling industry—to save the day. They have a stake in this. They're members of the community. They have to do their part. Right?

The trailer park, one of the few affordable-housing options left in Las Vegas, is endangered. The trailer park, our community without walls, is disappearing. The trailer park, a local icon, is dying.

"When we talk about the urbanization of Las Vegas, I think mobile-home parks are one of the things that will just go away," said Martin. "When we talk about high-rises and condos and things of that nature, mobile-home parks don't fit in. They'll be gone. They're a thing of the past."

NOTES FROM VEGAS UNDERGROUND

ON APRIL 4, 2002, IN A HOUSE IN DOWNTOWN LAS VEGAS, Timmy "T.J." Weber raped his girlfriend's daughter and killed his girlfriend and one of her sons. Police discovered the girlfriend's nude and bludgeoned body stuffed upside down in a storage container in a bedroom closet. A plastic bag secured with duct tape covered her head. Her son was found facedown on a mattress, his arms taped behind his back and a T-shirt stuffed in his mouth. He died of asphyxiation.

Following his carnival of crime, Weber left Las Vegas—but he soon returned. He ambushed his girlfriend's surviving son and an adult companion when they ventured to the family home to retrieve mementos for the funerals. Weber then fled on foot. He weaved around crumbling bungalows. He dashed across dirt yards, dogs barking in chorus. He climbed a barbwire fence surrounding a drainage ditch and disappeared into a storm drain.

Finally captured after more than three weeks on the run, Weber—who was featured on "America's Most Wanted"—told investigators that his journey through the storm-drain system reminded him of the movie *The Fugitive*. He spent five hours underground, he said, emerging between Interstate 15 and Palace Station (a hotel-casino more than three and a half miles upstream). He didn't indicate that he had a flashlight or that he'd previously explored the system.

Reading about Weber's escape route in the morning paper, I wondered how dark it was in the drain. What did he encounter down there? What were his thoughts? Was he scared? When he finally saw the light at the end of the tunnel, was he relieved?

I also wondered what I'd find if I traced Weber's trail. What lurks beneath Las Vegas? What secrets do the storm drains keep?

But this assignment wasn't designed for the managing editor of *CityLife*, I decided while shackled to my desk. Only the most daring and desperate mercenary would even *consider* it. Realizing this, I pitched the story to *CityLife* contributor Joshua Ellis, who'd displayed brass balls in his weekly column and a flair for first-person narratives in his feature stories. To my mild surprise, he accepted it.

But in a karmic twist, I became involved in the story. So with a hard hat on my head, a golf club in my hand, and Josh at my side, I wandered those dark and lonely corridors in search of what was described as a savage bearded beast.

ABANDON HOPE, ALL YE WHO ENTER HERE

BY JOSHUA ELLIS

If you slip through a crack in one of the walls along the west side of Main Street in downtown Las Vegas, you'll find yourself in the no-man's land between the red bricks of the Clark County Government Center and the Union Pacific railroad tracks, the blank back walls of hotel-casinos, and the elevated freedom of U.S. 95. It's a dusty wasteland filled with rubble and tumbleweeds, like the remnants of somebody's marriage. People live here, of course; people live anywhere they can, and there are worse places to bunk down for the night, believe me.

Head toward the U.S. 95 overpass, where it meets the train tracks, and you'll find a rectangle of chain-link fence. Inside the fence is a 20-foot-deep concrete hole with ladder rungs mounted on one side. Climb down the rungs and you'll see a two-tunnel storm drain leading off into darkness. There are 450 miles of flood channels in Clark County, 200 miles of which are underground. Nobody would want to hang out in these tunnels, it seems. They're dark and dangerous.

But I grew up in North Texas, a place where the rains come down hard for about five months out of the year, a place with millions of miles of culverts and drainage ditches and viaducts, the ultimate stage for a lonely kid to put on a one-man production of *Indiana Jones and the Temple of Doom*. I was never afraid of the tunnels.

It was pitch-black before freelance photographer Joel Lucas and I had gone 30 feet in one of the tunnels. But I'd brought a Mag-Lite, a heavy flashlight favored by cops. It functions as a powerful light source and a bludgeon and will keep working even after you smack some poor bastard over the head with it. My 18-inch kukri knife was stuck through my belt. We had no idea who or what might be lurking down there, and I really didn't want to be mugged by any random crackheads we might come across ... or killed for food by some deranged mutant, hideously scarred by nuclear testing in the 1950s and hiding in the dark ever since, emerging only to drag small animals and children into its terrible lair.

The chances of finding such a creature were unlikely, maybe ... but this *is* Las Vegas. The normal rules of reality end at the city limits.

Joel and I didn't encounter a single person the entire time we were in the tunnel, though. It appeared a few people were living in the tiny ledges of the manhole shafts—sleeping bags and shoes hung over the rungs that rose up to the street—but they were gone.

The tunnel was far too wet to sleep in. After the first mile or so, the floor was covered with two inches of scummy muddy water that stank like a corpse. There were cockroaches everywhere and albino fish spawning in the water by the thousands; they looked like deformed goldfish. Some of them were six inches long and too big to fit completely in the water, unable to swim and flopping slowly through the murk.

Even the most desperate vagrant would shudder at living in this dank hell ... a hell that never seemed to end, in fact, barreling into the distance beyond the beams of our flashlights. The silence was broken only by the sloshing of our boots and the occasional "thump-thump" of a car running over a manhole cover.

For a while, we kept up a stream of nervous conversation. But as the miles progressed, we lapsed into silence, listening only to the sound of our breath. And then we came across the first crawdaddy.

Crawdaddies—or crayfish or yabbies, depending on where you're from—

look sort of like midget lobsters; we used to find them in mud puddles after a big rain when I was a kid. It was a perennial spring preoccupation of Texan children to catch crawdaddies out of their mudholes and bring them to our mothers, who would make jambalaya with them. They're rarely more than four inches long, but this sonofabitch was about twice that size.

According to one Internet site, the largest North American crayfish species reaches a size of up to six inches—but they're only found in the White River basin of Missouri and Arkansas. Which leads to some obvious questions, none of which I have answers for.

Joel and I found more crawdaddies, hundreds or maybe thousands, blind and scuttling through the mud, living on rotted leaves and detritus from the streets.

And that was all. No (human) mutants, no fugitives hiding from the police, no vast network of mazelike catacombs. Just one tunnel, almost perfectly straight, leading on and on and on.

Eventually, Joel and I began to feel cool night air ... and finally we found ourselves standing in a wide swampy area next to an anonymous subdivision, being watched by a pack of middle school kids out for a walk. We asked them where we were and they told us we were near the corner of Sandhill Road and Washington Avenue. In three hours, we'd walked about five miles.

As we sat outside the 7-Eleven at Washington and Lamb Boulevard, waiting for our ride, I realized that our trip hadn't been in vain. There were secrets to be found, I was sure, somewhere in all those miles of manmade caves beneath the valley. Somewhere down there in the dark.

THERE'S A DARKNESS ON THE EDGE OF TOWN

Two weeks after pitching the story, I called Josh to see how the assignment was coming along. It was around noon, but I got the impression that I woke him. (Ah, the life of a freelancer!) He groggily explained that, accompanied by Joel and armed with the kukri knife, he'd explored a storm drain that began downtown and emptied into the Las Vegas Wash about five miles away. He and Joel didn't encounter anyone, but they did see sleeping bags and shoes hanging in manhole shafts—camps or storage spaces, he assumed, for street

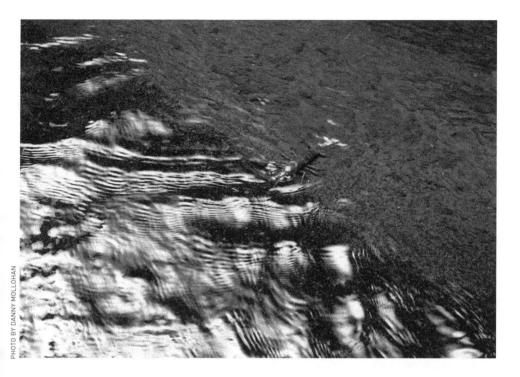

PHOTO BY DANNY MOLLOHAN

people living aboveground.

The drain was devastatingly dark, continued Josh in a morbid tone. He was now officially awake—and so was I. Scummy water covered the floor, and minnows spawned by the thousands. Six-inch-long crawfish—the biggest he'd ever seen (and he's from Texas, where everything is big)—nested in the crevices.

Intrigued, I asked Josh if he'd explored any other drains. He said that he hadn't, but he hoped to over the weekend. However, he added, "I may need a lift."

Anxious to place the story, I agreed to pick Josh up on Saturday morning. But before hanging up the phone, I explained that I would serve only as a chauffeur and that I had no intention of actually exploring the drains. The clothes I was wearing when I arrived at his house—a concert T-shirt, jeans, and casual work boots—further stressed my innocent-bystander role.

"You're not ready, man," said Josh, emerging from the house and looking me up and down.

"I'm not planning to go very far into the tunnels, if I go in at all," I said. "I'm just along for the ride, man."

In his right hand, Josh clutched the kukri knife and a Mag-Lite flashlight. A leather trench coat hung over his left arm. He was wearing a short-sleeve T-shirt, jeans, and black boots. Climbing back into my 1997 white-boy Camry, I pointed out that his outfit was no more elaborate than mine.

"I'll be fine," said Josh, flashing the kukri and a demented smile.

Since Josh lived in the southeast valley, we decided to search for storm drains rumored to be near the intersection of Boulder Highway and Russell Road. Blazing south on Boulder Highway, we passed trailer parks and neighborhood casinos, dive bars and no-cover-charge strip joints, and acres of desert that even the valley's insatiable developers had deemed useless. Just north of Russell, we crossed a wash. I tapped the brakes, pulled into a convenience store, and parked.

After walking across Russell and a plot of desert littered with beer cans, car tires, and Styrofoam cups, Josh and I pulled up at the edge of the wash. It was about 50 feet wide and 15 feet deep. A piss-colored creek wound through its bed. The wash rolled to the northeast about 500 feet, then snaked and disappeared. To the west, it cut under Boulder Highway and was swallowed by shrubs.

With no map, no drinking water, and no expectations, Josh and I crossed the snake-carcass-covered highway and followed the wash west along a chalky path. Josh complained bitterly about the heat—and with good reason. It was hotter than hell's kitchen. I looked around for rattlesnakes and dead bodies. This stretch of scorched earth—sand dunes, tumbleweeds, and cactuses (cattle skulls were the only thing missing)—could be home to nothing else, I'd already decided.

Around a bend, the wash transitioned into an open-air flood channel. Josh and I angled into the channel, discovering a six-foot-wide and four-foot-high tunnel in the west bank. As we approached the outlet, a shuffling sound shot from the darkness. We flinched, then identified ourselves as journalists. Echoes were the only response.

Confused, Josh and I crouched at the outlet and squinted into the tunnel. The floor was swept with sand. Official measurements, which looked like hieroglyphics to us, marked the walls. We had no idea if the tunnel was 50 feet or five miles long.

"I'm going to check it out," said Josh, snapping on the Mag-Lite.

"All right," I said, backing away from the outlet. I didn't even consider following him into the tunnel. It was low, dirty, and dark; I was tall, clean, and without a flashlight. There was no way in hell I was going to crawl into that glorified snake hole.

Handing me his trench coat, Josh shuffled sideways into the tunnel. His left hand held the flashlight. His right hand tickled the kukri, which dangled between his belt and the waist of his pants in the small of his back. He disappeared into the darkness. I heard shuffling, grunting, and cursing. Then there was silence.

I leaned into the tunnel. "Josh?" There was more shuffling, grunting, and cursing. Then Josh, dusty and sweaty, broke through the darkness.

"There's nothing down there," he said, breathing heavily. "It dead-ends. The sound we heard was an echo."

Exiting the tunnel, Josh collapsed on the bank. Sweat showed through his clothes and his chest rose and sank violently. I thought that he was going into cardiac arrest or something, that he was going to die right there on the glass-covered bank of a flood channel in southeast Vegas. What in the hell have I gotten myself into, I wondered? Isn't there a hard-hitting political story we could be covering? What are we doing here?

"Are you OK?" I asked Josh, glancing upstream. The channel tore northward for a quarter-mile, then swung to the west. "I'm going to jog ahead and see what's beyond the bend," I said. "I'll wave you on if there's anything interesting."

As I started upstream, two bicycles appeared around the bend. They weaved up and down the banks, cutting through the creek and leaving behind tire tracks. Finally, I could see that three boys were on the two bikes. One of them had blond spiky hair and appeared to be about 14. The other two, sharing a bike, looked like brothers—one about 12, the other eight.

"Do you all know if there are any tunnels around the bend?" I asked the boys.

They skidded to a stop and straddled the bikes. The blond pointed upstream. "Yeah," he said. "There's a big one back there. It's pretty long, I think. Some kids I know have gone in there, but not all the way."

"How far around the bend is it?"

"Not far."

I turned around and waved to Josh. He struggled to his feet, picked up his trench coat, and started upstream.

Rounding the bend, Josh and I saw the boys loitering in the shade of an overpass. The blond was straddling his bike. The other two were on foot, scurrying up and down the south bank like sewer rats. Drawing near, we noticed a gaping hole in the bank. It threatened to swallow the boys if they made one little misstep.

Crossing the creek, Josh and I approached the hole. It was more than five feet in diameter and cradled yellow-green standing water. It burrowed northward for about 30 feet, then jerked to the west. A pissy stench drifted from the darkness. To my surprise, the smallest boy scurried into the pipe. He quickly reemerged, wide-eyed and pale, as if he'd been greeted by a ghost.

"There's a flashlight in there that's on," he said.

"What?" I asked.

"Where?" said Josh.

"In the water."

Josh whipped out the kukri with a poetic flourish. The boys backed away from the pipe. Handing one of them his trench coat, he cut on the flashlight and approached the outlet with purpose. It was as if all of his energy had suddenly returned. I also felt reenergized. I mean, if there was "a flashlight in there that's on," as the boy had said, I wanted to see it.

To avoid stepping in the water, Josh and I walked with our legs spread and our feet on the sides of the pipe. This was terribly awkward—it looked like we were straddling invisible bulls—but better than sloshing through the muck, which was more than a foot deep in areas and appeared corrosive. We crashed through a cloud of mosquitoes, then stepped over a sunken milk carton, car battery, and flashlight (that wasn't on). Resting, I glanced between my legs. A reflection of the three boys peering into the pipe rippled in the water.

Negotiating the bend, legs cramping, Josh and I discovered a strange circular light in the water. We stared at it in awe. We couldn't make any sense of it. It seemed to shoot from the murky depths and actually pierce the top of the pipe. Is this the flashlight the boy was talking about? If not, what kind of bizarre alien beast is lurking beneath the surface?

Suddenly, there was a loud rush overhead. A metallic boom shook the pipe. Cowering, Josh and I noticed that the light disappeared and quickly reappeared in sync with the boom. We looked up, discovering a manhole shaft. A beam of sunlight angled through the cover's finger hole and dissolved into the water.

Realizing that a car had run over the manhole, Josh and I limped deeper into the pipe. He slashed through a cobweb with the kukri, the blade scraping against the concrete like a fingernail on a chalkboard. Goosebumps rose on my back and neck. About 50 feet beyond the bend, the water disappeared and the pipe narrowed to four feet. I glanced over my shoulder. The backlight had faded. Facing forward, I saw Josh's silhouette in the depths of the pipe.

"Slow down," I said. "I can't see shit."

Feeling like a hamster in plastic tubing, I finally caught up with Josh. The glow of the flashlight revealed that the pipe continued to narrow and appeared to climb into the heavens—no dead bodies, no live bodies, nothing.

After making the long walk back to the convenience store and finding refuge in an adjoining fast-food restaurant, Josh and I drove across town on Tropicana Avenue. The drive gave me time to reflect on our first exploration. We'd found very little in the pipe, I admitted: a car battery, a flashlight, a strange beam of sunlight. Certainly nothing newsworthy (though I was surprised by the foulness of the runoff that goes untreated into Lake Mead, the valley's main source of water). But, I realized, we *had* discovered an area of Las Vegas that few people—locals or tourists—knew anything about. In a city constantly featured in movies, TV shows, books, and articles, we'd stumbled on virgin territory—an underground world (literally and figuratively) that United Artists, E!, Frommer's, and *Maxim* had overlooked while focusing on poker rooms and the breasts of showgirls.

Encouraged by this realization, I turned south on Valley View Boulevard and parked on a side street. Josh and I opened the car doors and stepped out into the heat. Cursing Bugsy Siegel, Hank Greenspun, Howard Hughes, and all the other crazy white men who helped establish this city, we walked to a wash (which I'd discovered while researching a story on homelessness) and started downstream.

I'd, of course, seen storm drains throughout the valley. Some of them are visible from the streets and sidewalks; others can be seen from the washes, which also serve as recreation areas (though I wouldn't recommend walking a dog or throwing a frisbee in any of the central channels). But I'd never paid attention to the drains. I didn't know their official name. I didn't know their specific purpose. They were just another part of the valley's sprawling infrastructure that I took for granted, just another thing in this world that I unconsciously ignored.

But standing in front of it with Josh, I couldn't ignore *this* storm drain. Its face was white, clean, and 10 feet tall. Its walls were smooth and strong, making it look more like a sculpture buried in dirt than some kind of flood channel.

Josh and I had no idea who or what waited in the dark—but he wasn't taking any chances. He drew the kukri, wriggled into the trench coat, and tied its belt tight. We then ducked into the south tunnel of the storm drain, discovering two men sitting in the shade surrounded by empty beer bottles. Surprised—though probably not as surprised as the men, considering Josh's startling silhouette—we explained that we were journalists curious about what was in the drain. Nothing really, said the men. It's just a refuge for people who live in the wash. It gets too hot out there. But no one actually lives in the drain, they said. It's way too dangerous. That floodwater comes like a thief in the night. It will take you away and won't ever bring you back.

After talking to the men briefly, Josh and I shuffled deeper into the drain. The dividing wall disappeared, yielding to an arching tunnel 20 feet wide and five feet high at its apex. Sand and rocks were scattered across the floor. The walls and ceiling were remarkably clean.

About 300 feet downstream, Josh and I discovered another divider. It created two 10-by-5 tunnels that straightened into perfect darkness. Josh aimed the flashlight into the north tunnel, which was cluttered with rocks and blocks of concrete—testaments to the awesome power of floodwater. We considered exploring the south tunnel, which was less cluttered than the north, but ultimately decided against it. We assumed that the tunnel was long, low, and dark. We assumed that it was crawling with spiders, scorpions, and maybe even snakes. We assumed that it was suicide.

THERE'S A WORLD GOING ON UNDERGROUND

BY JOSHUA ELLIS

"Come on, man," Matt said. "One more stop and we're done."

I glared at him as I huddled in the passenger seat of the car, dripping with sweat, watching the strip malls and neon bars go by. After escaping the pipe off Boulder Highway, we'd just emerged from the storm drain near Tropicana and Valley View. We were heading west on Tropicana.

"All right," I said. "But we're going to have to go to Café Espresso Roma after this. I need a fucking iced mocha."

We pulled into the Home Depot at Trop and Decatur Boulevard, which lay opposite another storm drain Matt knew about. We stepped out into the heat. I'm *such* a pussy when it comes to a summer afternoon in the high desert. Walking out into the daylight in June in Las Vegas is like having a dragon breathe on you; the air feels and smells like roasting shit.

We crossed the road and headed down into a drainage ditch.

This was the biggest drain we'd seen so far, at least 30 feet wide and 10 feet high. It was split into three tunnels, separated by thick concrete walls. The middle tunnel was clogged with refuse and mud and shit, but the south tunnel was open and inviting. As we walked into it, we heard sounds from inside: rustling, whispering ... or maybe even footsteps.

There's a valley in central Turkey called Cappadocia, where ancient Christians dug hundreds of miles of catacombs to hide from the Romans, who were quite intent on nailing them to trees. Some of these catacombs run for 30 miles or more. As you crawl through them, you find friezes of the Virgin Mary and the occasional coin with the face of Augustus—strange reminders that some poor bastard actually *lived* here, hiding from the Man (personified in the third century by the local Roman legion).

Looking into the tunnel, it wasn't hard to imagine what it might have been like to be the poor sonofabitch centurion who had to go into the catacombs and roust the Christians. Standing at the mouth of a cave, listening to the inhabitants move about. Christ. It doesn't matter how old you are or how well-adjusted you may be. You *will* be afraid of the dark.

Matt and I made no particular effort to be quiet as we headed deeper into the tunnel; for obvious reasons, we didn't want to sneak up on anybody.

Matt called out, "We're journalists doing a story on the tunnels. Is anyone here?"

I asked him to be quiet; I had a feeling that anybody down there would probably want to talk to a journalist about as much as they'd want to talk to a cop. I didn't think anybody was going to greet us with open arms.

We both jumped when we came upon the first inhabitant, 500 feet into the tunnel, curled in a fetal position on a homemade bed, hands covering face.

"We're reporters interviewing people about living in the drainage tunnels," Matt said. "Can we talk to you for a minute?"

The shape kept its hands resolutely over its face and didn't speak. It was impossible to tell if it were a man or woman; the lumpy unidentifiable clothing and ragged long hair didn't give any clues.

"Are you OK?" O'Brien asked. Nothing.

Matt and I continued downstream. About 1,000 feet into the drain, we discovered three holes in the tunnel's north wall that looked like hobbit doorways. We found out later they're called "equalizers"; they allow water to flow from one tunnel to another, equalizing the levels. Leaning down and looking through them, we could see that another set of holes led into the north tunnel.

"Hello?" said Matt. "Anyone there?" He leaned down and stuck his head through one of the holes.

"Don't do that," I said. I was getting strange vibes all of a sudden and was nervous. "Let's just keep going down this way."

"I want to look in here real quick," Matt said. He crawled through the hole and bounced the flashlight beam off the walls of the middle tunnel. "There's nobody here."

But there *was* somebody there. I knew it—but I didn't say anything about it, partly because I didn't want to freak out O'Brien and partly because I didn't want to sound like a nervous little bitch.

Matt and I didn't go much farther. The ceiling of the tunnel dropped sharply, until it was about four and a half feet high. We could see that the tunnel kept going beyond the range of the flashlight, but we couldn't tell if the ceiling got any higher. I told Matt that after the earlier events of the day, I was too trashed to walk hunched over for a mile or two in what could easily turn into a dead end.

As we turned around, I heard a splash behind us, farther down the tunnel. It sounded like a foot stepping into a puddle.

"Did you hear that?" I asked Matt.

"What?"

"Somebody's down there," I said. "Let's get the hell out of here."

Matt and I started walking briskly; we weren't running, but we weren't lounging around the place either. When we reached the equalizers, we crawled through them into the north tunnel.

"Do you smell that?" asked Matt, as we began back toward the inlet. The air was heavy with the smell of smoke. "This is *strange*," he said—and I had to agree.

We kept walking upstream. The tunnel turned to the south.

"Holy shit!" said one of us. Or maybe it was both of us.

A dozen or so shopping carts covered with upholstery lined the tunnel's south wall.

"Ellis, what *is* this?" asked Matt.

"It's the fucking Blair Witch, man. I have no idea."

We slowed down, playing the flashlight over the carts. I couldn't make out much of what was in them: One contained a leather satchel, another the head of an electric broom nestled in unidentifiable trash. There were shoes and jackets and broken household appliances and cardboard boxes and God only knows what else. We certainly didn't take inventory.

The carts were placed in a perfect row against the wall, as if still in front of the supermarket. And beyond the carts was the hut.

Imagine a kid's playhouse made of pine wood: three walls, a ceiling, and an Army blanket for a curtain. Imagine that it's surrounded by folded clothing, bicycles, shopping carts, car batteries, and Coleman lamps. Imagine that a cinder-block fire pit sits alongside it.

Matt and I suddenly understood where the smoke was coming from. The ceiling and the top of the walls were black with soot. I angled the Mag-Lite into the hut. Inside were two men sleeping on a futon mattress, wearing only boxer shorts.

I was in a state of complete mental disorientation—not fear, but something close to cultural panic.

"There are people in there!" I said to Matt. "Let's get the hell out of here!"

We crept past the hut. At the front border of the camp, a piece of rebar was wedged between the tunnel walls like the velvet rope of a nightclub. As I ducked under it, it caught on my trench coat and scraped across the walls.

A voice shot from the darkness. "Who's there?" There were fumbling sounds.

"Sorry," I said.

"We're reporters," said Matt. "We were just passing through."

A pale form emerged from the darkness. "You see how clean it is here? If you want us to leave, we will."

"Oh, no," I said quickly. "We're just journalists. We're doing a story about people living in the drainage tunnels."

The shape took form as a thin, bearded man. His hair was rumpled and he was rubbing the sleep out of his eyes. "We keep everything very clean," he insisted, as if he thought we were some kind of inspectors.

"We're with *CityLife* newspaper," O'Brien said. "I'm Matt. This is Josh."

"I'm Ron," said the man, extending his hand.

Matt shook it and asked, "How long have you lived down here?"

"About a year," said another sleepy voice. "Who are you guys again?"

We repeated that we were journalists researching a story.

"That's John," said Ron. We could see John's silhouette sitting on the edge of the mattress, lighting a cigarette.

It turned out that Ron and John had lived in the drain for 15 months. They worked odd jobs during the day and returned to the tunnel at night. They cooked meat in the fire pit. They pissed in Double Big Gulp cups, which they emptied outside. They swept and cleaned the tunnel as if it were a suburban tract home.

"Does Metro ever mess with you?" I asked.

"No," said Ron. "They know we're in here. They come and check on us, make sure we're OK, every so often."

"What about flooding?" I continued. "This tunnel must fill up quickly when it rains."

"Metro comes and warns us," Ron said.

"Sorry to sneak up on you guys," said Matt. "We didn't know anybody was in here. We were farther back in the drain, just looking around."

"Did you see the troll?" asked Ron, matter-of-factly.

"The *troll*?" Matt repeated.

"Yeah, there's a troll that lives back there," said Ron. "He's been back there forever. But he doesn't mess with us and we don't mess with him."

"He can see in the dark!" John added.

Matt and I fell silent.

"He's been living back there forever and has a real long beard," continued Ron. "You don't want to run into him. He can see in the dark. He hides from people. We were walking down there one time and we thought we heard something. I looked into one of those holes in the wall and there he was, looking right at me."

"You're shitting me," I said.

"Nope," said Ron. "He was carrying a crowbar and he swung it at me."

"A *crowbar*?" asked Matt.

"Yeah," said Ron. "You don't want to surprise him. He'll bash you with it."

"I *knew* it," I said. "I *knew* I heard someone back there."

"He's fucking crazy," said John. "Hey, does one of you have a cigarette?"

After talking to Ron and John for 10 or 15 minutes, Matt and I scurried out of the drain and back to the car. We were horrified, exhilarated, and—most of all—curious. A troll who lives in the depths of a storm drain? A long beard? A crowbar? Could any of this possibly be true? Or were Ron and John just fucking with us, so we'd stay away from their home? Either way, it didn't matter. Matt and I had a dramatic conclusion to our story: We'd return to the drain the next day and search for the troll.

NO ONE SHOULD BRAVE THE UNDERWORLD ALONE

Following a night of fragmented sleep, I woke early the next morning. I rolled onto my back and stared at the ceiling. For more than 18 hours, I'd been unable to shake the image of the troll—stringy hair, scraggly beard, hairy chest, bent back, and pale skin. I imagined Charles Manson after 15 years of hard storm-drain living.

After showering, I drove to Home Depot. I roamed its marathon aisles for more than an hour, finally emerging with an armful of items that included a hard hat, headlight, Mag-Lite, Mini Mag-Lite, clothesline, snap hook, four-pack of AA batteries, and four-pack of D batteries. The cashier eyed the items suspiciously.

"I'm doing some underground work today," I explained, as I handed her my debit card. "Just want to make sure I'm prepared."

Next, I drove to an EZ Pawn. I'd put considerable thought into what weapon to take back into the drain, but had yet to be inspired. A stroll through a pawnshop would spark my imagination, I figured. Since Josh and I'd ruled out a gun, noting the ricochet factor and the amplified acoustics, I headed straight to the knives section. It was woefully depleted.

"Do you carry any swords?" I asked a salesman in a professional tone.

"Nah," he answered, as if ashamed. "I'm sorry. We don't."

On my way out of the pawnshop, I cut through the sports section. There, amid scuffed-up fishing poles and pool sticks, I came across a bag of golf clubs. A seven-iron, I immediately realized, was the perfect weapon to take into the drain. It could be used as a walking stick, to flip debris out of my way, to knock down spider webs, and to test the depth of water. It wasn't as intimidating as, say, a chainsaw and it had at least a foot on any crowbar I'd seen.

When I picked up Josh at 7 p.m. (we'd decided to enter the drain at nightfall to add to the drama), I was wearing a long-sleeve T-shirt, cargo pants, and combat boots. He was dressed in the trench coat, a black tee, black jeans, and black boots—storm-drain gothic. As he climbed into the Camry, I handed him a sheet of paper.

"Sign this," I said, cranking up the Stones and backing out of the driveway. It was a disclaimer, hastily written after a conversation with the company attorney. It read, "I, Joshua Ellis, enter this dark and mazelike storm drain on my own accord. I am researching this story without editorial direction or pressure from *Las Vegas CityLife* or its parent company, Wick Communications. The publication is *not* responsible for any foul or evil misfortune that may befall me during the research. Right hand raised, Joshua Ellis."

I'd written the disclaimer mainly for effect, to fuck with Josh, to get a reaction. And indeed, it did. He smiled uncomfortably as he read it, as if reviewing his own will, and a bead of sweat splashed down on the sheet. After attempting and failing to secure a higher word rate, he signed it reluctantly.

Fifteen minutes later, I pulled into the Home Depot opposite the storm drain. *CityLife* Photo Editor Bill Hughes, who'd agreed to follow us into the drain after two freelancers backed out of the assignment, was waiting in his truck, sucking on a cigarette. I jumped out of the car and opened the back door; a waterfall of gear spilled to the asphalt. I picked up the Mag-Lite and put it in a top pocket of my pants. I dropped the Mini Mag-Lite into a side pocket, then picked up a piece of clothesline, threaded it through the eye of the snap hook, and tied it loosely around my neck. I looped the string handle of my tape recorder over the hook. The hard hat found my head. Finally, I gripped the iron and took a few wild practice swings.

"Fore, motherfuckers!" I yelled, prepared to go Tiger Woods on anyone and anything in the drain.

Following a photo session at the inlet, Josh and I entered the north tunnel. Bill, weighed down with gear, followed closely. We immediately encountered two men and a woman sharing a 32-ounce bottle of beer.

"Do you think we'll find anything back there?" I asked them.

Matt and Josh

"If you're talking about dead people, no," said one of the men.

"We're talking about people *living* back there."

"Just the two guys who live up the way, but they're not home. I don't know where they're at."

"Ron and John?"

"Yeah. You know them?"

"We talked to them yesterday." I paused. Then risking ridicule, I asked, "Do you know anything about a troll who lives in the drain?"

"A troll?" said the man. "Nah, that's bullshit."

"There aren't any weird fuckers living back there?" asked Josh.

"Fuck no."

"That's what Ron and John told us," Josh said.

"You can't believe anything those guys say. There ain't nobody back there."

Josh and I started off into the darkness, Bill trailing. Reaching the front of Ron and John's camp, we called out their names. There was no response. Cautiously, we ducked under the curtain and approached the hut. The bikes were gone, the hut was empty, and the ashes of the grill were dead and dusty. I suggested that we wait for Ron and John to return, so we could question them further about the drain and the troll—but Josh surged downstream. Bill and I followed him. Approaching the equalizers, he finally slowed down.

"Anyone home?" I asked, kneeling in front of one of the holes.

"Anyone home? Anyone home? Anyone home?"

"We're journalists exploring the storm drains. We're not looking for any trouble."

"We're journalists exploring the storm drains. We're not looking for any trouble."

Josh squeezed through one of the equalizers. It didn't sound as if he got crowbarred to death by a heinous troll, so Bill and I followed him. The three of us then looped into a wide arching tunnel. Josh cut off his flashlight.

"Matt," he said, "cut your flashlight off." I did, and the tunnel went dark. "Do you hear that?"

A faint ticking sound echoed in the tunnel. It sounded like a drip or maybe even a clock. I cut on my flashlight and inched downstream. The ticking got louder, but I couldn't place it. It seemed to be coming from all directions.

Bill bailed out, explaining that he wanted to see if Ron and John had returned. Josh and I continued downstream. The ticking got louder and louder. Finally, the beams of our flashlights met on a wind-up clock that was wedged between a rock and a wet piece of cloth. I picked up the clock and wiped off its face. It read 9:35 p.m. I removed my cell phone from a pocket: 9:35 p.m.

"Tick, tick, tick."

LONG IS THE WAY AND HARD, THAT OUT OF HELL LEADS UP TO LIGHT
BY JOSHUA ELLIS

Matt and I worked our way over to the storm drain's south tunnel and continued downstream. The ceiling rose and sank like a rollercoaster. The low area where we'd turned around the day before only went on for about 100 feet, then the ceiling rose again. The tunnel angled sharply to the north. There was smoke in the air—but it wasn't coming from Ron and John's camp.

Matt stuck his head through an equalizer.

"I think the smoke's coming from in there," he said. He ducked through the equalizer and turned upstream in the middle tunnel. I followed him. The smell of smoke grew stronger.

"Look at that!" said Matt, amazed.

A bowling ball splattered with mud sat in the middle of the floor. Matt and I froze and stared at the ball as if it were a witch's head. Honestly, we didn't know *what* to make of this. Perhaps someone had accidentally rolled the ball down a drop inlet, thrown a gutter ball—literally. Or maybe a flood had washed it into the drain. Those, of course, were the logical explanations. But why had the ball stopped there, in the middle of the tunnel, unimpeded? And was it a coincidence that the finger holes were facing up?

Questions without answers. That, it seems, is what Matt and I found in the storm drains of Las Vegas.

"A souvenir," I said, picking up the ball.

"You're going to carry that thing all the way through the drain?" asked Matt.

"Yeah. Why not? I could always take up bowling."

Continuing upstream in the tunnel, Matt and I discovered the ashes of a campfire. A tombstone-shaped piece of plywood, which apparently served as a bed, lay next to the ashes. A piece of rebar stretched across the wood.

"That looks a hell of a lot like a crowbar," stammered Matt, flashlight fixed on the rebar. Then he announced, "We're journalists. We're not here to mess with anyone. We're just looking around."

"We're average American citizens, like yourself," I muttered.

Kukri knife and golf club poised, we entered a low and wide chamber. Ghoulish graffiti covered the walls. Through equalizers, we could see into dark and spacious side rooms.

"I'm going to have a cigarette," I said, collapsing against a wall. I set the trench coat, knife, and bowling ball in a pile and lit up.

"This area is creepy, man," said Matt, sitting next to me and angling the beam of his flashlight through an equalizer. The interior of the drain was a concrete labyrinth, with pipes and tunnels and chambers leading in all directions. Its Minotaur was nearby. Matt and I could sense the beast just beyond the range of our flashlights.

"Hey, listen," I said. "We know you're in here. We're not going to bother you. We're just doing a story for a newspaper. If you want to talk, cool. We'll get your story out to the public. If you don't want to talk, that's all right. We won't bother you."

Silence ensued. Apparently, whoever or whatever lived in this area of the drain wasn't interested in publicity. He, she, or it probably had enough problems without the press snooping around.

After hanging out in the chamber for 10 minutes, Matt and I continued downstream. We ducked through an equalizer and found ourselves in a long tunnel. Finally, as we turned a corner, we saw a dim light in the distance. The silhouette of a man sitting on a milk crate broke the light. As we approached, he looked at us with a remarkable lack of surprise.

"Hey," said Matt, "we're reporters from *CityLife*. How's it going?"

"Fair," the man replied laconically.

PHOTO BY DANNY MOLLOHAN

Eddie

"Sorry to bother you," continued Matt. "We walked all the way from the other end of the drain."

Matt extended his hand and introduced himself.

"I'm Eddie," said the man, shaking Matt's hand. Eddie glanced at the recorder dangling from Matt's neck. "You're not videotaping this, are you?"

"No," said Matt. "It's a tape recorder."

I offered Eddie a cigarette, but he declined. The transcript picked up the conversation from there:

MATT: When's the last time you had traffic coming from the direction we just came from?

EDDIE: Anybody at all?

MATT: Yeah.

EDDIE: [Pause] I'd say about four days.

JOSH: The guys at the other end of the tunnel said they hadn't had any traffic coming from this direction in more than three months.

EDDIE: I'm surprised to hear that. A lot more people enter the tunnels from that end than this end. They see a lot more traffic than I do. That wash on the other end is like a recreation area. A lot of people come in the tunnels down there, but don't come all the way through.

JOSH: The guys at the other end said—and I quote—there's a "troll" living in there, a guy who hasn't left the tunnels for years and can see in the dark.

EDDIE: That's possible, but I've never seen him.

Understandably, Eddie was nervous. I'm six-foot-four in boots and weigh about 300 pounds. Matt is six-foot-four and weighs about 200 pounds. I was carrying a bowling ball and a knife that could gut a shark. Matt was clutching a seven-iron. We appeared at Eddie's back door, as it were, breathing heavily and sweating like galley slaves. He had every right to assume we were madmen, assassins hired by the casino industry to get rid of the riffraff.

But Eddie eventually relaxed. He told us he was a "gambling degenerate" who'd lived in the drain for about a year and a half. He even gave us a tour of his camp.

Suddenly, a clean-cut man in a white T-shirt and denim shorts emerged from the depths of the drain.

"I think you woke my friend up," said Eddie.

The man, who refused to give his name, told us he moved into the drain because of an unsatisfactory home life. He'd been in there for only a few days, he said. His boss picked him up at a nearby restaurant in the morning and dropped him off at the restaurant at night.

I flashed back to the manholes I'd seen on my first exploration of the underworld and the sleeping bags and shoes perched on concrete ledges no more than two feet wide. People live there. People will live anywhere—cardboard boxes, underpasses, vacant lots, dumpsters, storm drains. Life always finds a way, even if it's a way most of us can't imagine.

I thought about the troll living in the perpetual midnight of the tunnels. How did he eat? How did he drink? How did he survive? More questions without answers.

Time to go. Matt and I'd had enough. We couldn't take any more darkness, drama, and confusion. We mumbled our goodbyes to Eddie and his friend and began down a low tunnel, toward the light. Finally, we ducked out of the drain.

The sun had fallen behind the mountains and the eastern sky was dark.

In front of us, across Industrial Road and I-15, stood Bellagio and Caesars Palace, awash in neon. The "fabulous" Las Vegas Strip, where so many dreams are found and lost. The Strip, where it's never really nighttime at all.

BELLY OF THE BEAST

EVERY NOW AND THEN, when life gets complicated and the weasels start closing in, the only real cure is to put on a leather trench coat, clutch an 18-inch kukri knife, and wander around in the storm drains of Las Vegas. To relax, as it were, in the womb of the desert. Just put on a hard hat, grip a seven-iron, and plunge through the black curtains and find out what bizarre scenes are being performed on the concrete stage.

With apologies to Hunter S. Thompson, whose classic *Fear and Loathing in Las Vegas* is paraphrased above, that's what freelance writer Joshua Ellis and I did earlier this summer. Our story, published in *CityLife*, received a surprising amount of attention and Josh and I received hundreds of e-mails, alternately detailing our brilliance and cowardice.

"I just wanted the two of you to know that in my 53 years, I have read a lot of newspaper stories that grabbed me and held me ... and your story on life under the streets is right up there," read one e-mail.

"You guys are *such* pussies!" read another.

Some of the e-mails suggested a follow-up story.

While averse to gratuitous follow-ups, Josh and I decided that a second story made sense. The first story spawned several questions that weren't answered, two of which seem particularly intriguing:

What did fugitive Timmy "T.J." Weber encounter in the storm-drain system? And what secrets do the storm drains under the Strip keep?

A return trip to the drains answered these questions, in part. Lace up your boots. Put on your hard hat. And don't forget your flashlight.

DIG ME DOWN DEEP WHERE THE DEAD MEN SLEEP

BY JOSHUA ELLIS

July Fourth and Las Vegas was celebrating by being hot as hell's parking lot.

Matt and I pulled into a convenience store across from the Rio. Penn & Teller stared down at us from the hotel-casino's video-screen sign, like gods in gray suits. Across Interstate 15, the Strip gleamed in the harsh light. Time to park and get out of the heat. Time to go back into the dark.

Matt and I discovered a six-tunnel storm drain that ran under Industrial Road, the interstate, and presumably the Strip. It lay at the end of a nasty dribbling wash that bordered a row of office buildings. As we entered one of the drain's middle tunnels in our traditional gear, the air grew cooler and less humid. The tunnel was dry as a bone—hardly surprising, since it had last rained in February.

But when the rain comes down on the Mojave Desert, it comes like God's judgment, tear-assing over the hard terrain and into the streets. These tunnels were designed to handle floodwater, theoretically. But it never quite works that way—which is why the valley nearly drowned in July 1999, when three inches of rain fell in an hour and a half.

Matt and I had walked about a half-mile in the tunnel when the air got warmer and we saw sunlight—which was odd, since we'd determined we were under the interstate. The drain's six tunnels opened into a chamber, which was at least 60 feet wide and 25 feet long. On the opposite side of the chamber, two massive tunnels barreled into the darkness. Above us was a large grate. Sunlight poured through it perfectly. And the walls came alive with symbols, words, and images.

A portrait of a giant blue wasp, done in hyper-realistic 3-D, floated on an off-white plane. Its caption read, "Diagram for Self-Destruction." Different parts of the wasp's anatomy were labeled: "Just Know/That We/Must Learn/

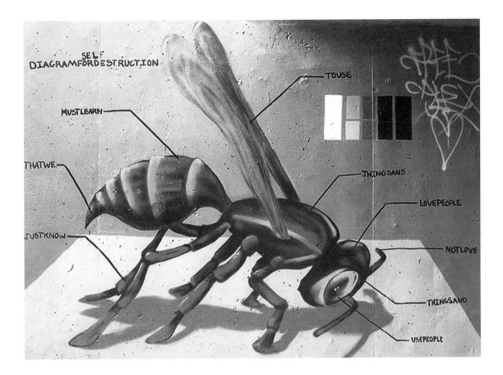

to Use/Things and/Love People/Not Love/Things and/Use People." Next to the wasp was a portrait of a young man with a stone face and Caesar haircut. Its legend read, "Embrace Truth in a World of Lies."

Graffiti tags covered the walls: colorful names and phrases, anime characters, scary monsters, and super creeps, as bright and shiny as the feathers of an angel's wing.

"There *is* culture in Las Vegas," said Matt. "It's just all underground."

The gallery was the most beautiful thing I'd seen in Las Vegas, maybe the only beautiful thing. Vegas loves the spectacle, but there's little here that displays even a modicum of taste or thought—just endless neon and vapid stucco palaces, surrounded by a dusty hardpan desert as ugly as an old whore.

As Matt and I explored the art gallery, we noticed an encampment upstream in one of the tunnels. It consisted of a stool, cooler, and cardboard hut that looked like a jet-fighter cockpit. We couldn't tell if anyone was inside the hut.

"Hello?" said Matt.

"We're journalists from *CityLife,*" I said. "If there's anybody in there, we just want to talk about the art on the walls. It's beautiful."

There was no response.

Matt and I cut back through the art gallery and started down one of the massive tunnels. Something on the ceiling caught my eye: a fluorescent light fixture, covered with graffiti, the bulbs broken out or stolen long ago. Farther downstream, there were halogen lamps, also broken out.

"Come look at this," I said to Matt, who was studying the seemingly never-ending graffiti on the walls. "Why would there be a light fixture in here? I mean, this tunnel fills with water, right? This can't be a drainage tunnel. Drainage tunnels don't have lights in them."

"I don't know what's going on," said Matt, obviously confused. "These *are* drainage tunnels; I'm sure of that. I saw them on the Flood Control District's map."

We studied some tubing that ran along the south wall. It was open in areas and multicolored wires (data or phone lines, from what I could gather) coiled out. Deeper into the tunnel, a busted junction box was bolted to the ceiling. I flicked open my knife and held the blade to a wire.

"Do you have any idea what I could do to the Strip right now?" I asked Matt. "Just one snap. Are the casinos really this stupid? Didn't anybody watch *Ocean's Eleven*?"

"I'm surprised we were able to just walk right in here," said Matt. "You'd think there would be some security on the Fourth of July, considering there were terrorist threats against the city. Fuck, man. We'll probably get blown to bits by a dirty bomb down here."

"Fuck terrorists," I said. "They should worry about me. Give me an ax. I'll take the whole city down."

"Osama?" called out Matt, as we continued deeper into the drain. "Elvis? Mr. Hoffa?"

Matt and I walked for a long time; it was hard to tell exactly how long, but at least another half-mile. The hieroglyphics on the walls had degenerated from the colorful landscape of the art gallery into sullen scrawls: "Fuck All Nazis" and "RIP Spit and Dan." Farther into the drain, "Kill Jew Faggots." Declarations of love and hate, peace and murder, both sides of the coin, the sickness and hatred and desperation that paint every stroke of the Las Vegas canvas.

"What's that noise?" asked Matt.

The sound of rushing water grew louder.

"Oh shit," I said. "I know what it is. What sits right in front of the Bellagio?"

"The fake lake?"

"Hell yeah, the lake!"

"Let's get the hell out of here," said Matt. "It sounds like a torrent down there. We could get killed." Yet we continued downstream.

As we came around a bend, we both stopped—eyes wide open. An iron pipe four feet in diameter punched a hole in the wall. The pipe was covered with a lid ... a completely useless lid, as water poured out of the pipe and flooded the floor.

"You think it's the lake?" asked Matt, sweeping the beam of his flashlight across the water.

"Or the fountains in front of Caesars Palace," I said. "We're under the Strip."

The tunnel split into four smaller tunnels, each filled with about three inches of water. Matt and I ducked into the north tunnel. Ahead of us was light. At first, I couldn't make sense of what I was seeing: a low-ceilinged room supported by concrete columns. It looked like an underground parking lot.

"Where are we?" I said, as we stumbled into a wide chamber.

"Somewhere we're not supposed to be," said Matt.

THERE IS A LIGHT THAT NEVER GOES OUT

Seeing the light, Josh and I were utterly confused. We'd expected the drain to tunnel all the way under the Strip, then empty into a wash or an open-air channel. We couldn't make any sense of what we were seeing: columns, a low ceiling, fluorescent lights. At the far end of the chamber, natural light burned behind a sectioned wall.

How could we be seeing light so soon, I wondered? How could we be seeing light so close to the Strip?

Anxious to figure out where we were, Josh and I slalomed through the columns. We sidestepped a grate that swallowed most of the runoff oozing from the blackness behind us. The ceiling rose and the natural light grew brighter. A section of the wall was held open by chains, revealing passing cars and pedestrians.

"We're under the Imperial Palace!" I said, recognizing the casino's distinct driveway.

"Holy shit!" said Josh. "You're right!"

As Josh and I approached the sectioned wall, a man in an Imperial Palace work uniform appeared on the driveway. He seemed startled when my voice shot from the shadows.

"'Is this driveway a flood channel?" I asked the man.

"Yeah," he said, stopping and squinting at me and Josh. "The water runs onto the driveway and is carried all the way to the back of the hotel."

"What about the traffic?"

"We stop traffic at the valet garage when it rains."

"Do you know of any other drains that go under the Strip?"

"No. I think this is the main one."

Josh and I exited the chamber and followed the driveway to the back of the hotel. On the far side of a crossroad, behind a guardrail, was another drain. Its inlet was gated and a sign above it read, "Warning No Trespassing Flood Channel."

Josh and I turned around. We walked back up the driveway, ducked into the chamber, and began our return journey through the drain in the other massive tunnel. Cockroaches crawled along the walls like liquid graffiti. Lateral pipes puked water onto the floor.

"This is a dungeon, man," I said, "an absolute dungeon."

I half-expected to stumble on overweight showgirls and reject lounge acts chained to the walls, being whipped by pit bosses in leather bondage gear, but found nothing of the sort. Only racist graffiti and a nook leading up to sunlight. Josh leaned into the nook.

"Excuse me," he said. "Can anyone tell me where the casino is? I seem to have taken a wrong turn."

As Josh and I approached a fleet of triangular columns, the tunnel went dark and deadly silent. There were hundreds of thousands of people somewhere overhead, but all we could hear were chirping crickets. Wild-style graffiti covered every inch of the walls, creating one seemingly never-ending scroll of words.

Since we were under Caesars Palace, I was tempted to compare

the drain to the catacombs of Rome. These catacombs, dug beginning in the second century A.D. and stretching for more than 60 miles, served as houses of worship for Jews and early Christians who were persecuted aboveground and as a necropolis for their martyrs and saints. To this day, funerary art adorns the walls. Faded paintings, friezes, and mosaics pay homage to Christian icons, symbols, and practices. Sculptures and altars lurk in the shadows.

But actually, the drain—which was anything but sacred—reminded me more of the quarries of Paris than the catacombs of Rome. (By the way, the Paris hotel-casino is just 500 feet south of this drain.) The digging of the quarries began around the 12th century A.D. The limestone, gypsum, and clay provided the raw materials needed to build the city, including Notre Dame, the Louvre, and the Bastille. (The limestone was used to make buildings, the gypsum to make plaster, and the clay to make bricks and tiles.) But after six centuries of digging, the bedrock was full of holes. Worried about the stability of the city, the council of King Louis XVI commissioned a study on the condition of the quarries. The findings were so alarming that the council created an agency to map out and stabilize the underground. The agency was divided into two groups: one dug inspection galleries, which allowed workers to explore the earth and search for quarries; the other mapped and stabilized them.

Over the past four centuries, a stunning collection of art has accumulated in the quarries and inspection galleries beneath Paris. The earliest known marking is dated 1609; the most recent was made yesterday. The art was created over a period of time that includes the storming of the Bastille (1789), the Great Terror of the revolution (1794), the Prussian siege of 1870, the German occupation of 1940, and the subsequent liberation. It was left by an array of people: engineers, quarrymen, Prussian and German soldiers, artists, tourists, and street people.

Some of the art's official, some of it's illicit. It includes inscriptions (e.g., the date on which a quarry was stabilized), directional signs, graffiti, sculptures, mosaics, and installations. The subject matter is ridiculous (politics) and sublime (soft porn). Concerts and festivals have been held in the quarries, subversive films shown on the walls. There's even a tombstone down there, which marks the spot where Philibert Aspairt was found and buried.

Aspairt, the doorkeeper of the Val-de-Grace hospital, made a secret solo descent into the underground in 1793 (apparently in search of wine that was stored in the cellars). He never emerged. In the turbulent times of the revolution, his disappearance caused little (if any) concern. But in 1804, a group of surveyors found a leather belt and rat-gnawed bones beneath the Val-de-Grace. A set of keys helped identify the remains as the hospital's former doorkeeper, who'd disappeared so many years ago.

Reality and myth merge in the quarries … and like the light and dark, it's tough to tell where one ends and the other begins. Rumor has it Marat found refuge in the underground during the revolution. Apparently, Charles X threw parties in the catacombs before the revolution of 1830. And Balzac is said to have escaped his creditors by using the mazelike 180 miles of tunnels.

Unfortunately, they all resisted the urge to write their names on the walls.

While trying to read the names on the walls of the storm drain (Wayne Newton? Steve Wynn? Tony "The Ant" Spilotro?), Josh and I were nearly decapitated by a water pipe that ran across the ceiling. The pipe was a foot in diameter, rusted, and tangled with cobwebs. It didn't appear to be a sprinkler-system line. In fact, it looked more like a water main connecting two of Caesars Palace's many towers.

Finally, Josh and I reached the art gallery. He asked to borrow my cell phone. I tossed it to him, then collapsed on the floor.

"We're OK," I overheard Josh tell his mom. "Yeah, we're fine. Look, I got to go. There's another tunnel here I want to check out." He paused. "I'll be fine. I'll call you when I get out, OK?"

Josh handed the phone back to me and began raking debris from the outlet of a lateral pipe. Less than four feet in diameter, the pipe was crooked as lightning and appeared to jerk for miles.

"What are you going in there for?" I asked him.

"I want to check it out," he said.

"There's nothing in there, man."

Josh set his flashlight on the floor and took off his trench coat. "Hold this," he said, handing me the coat. "I'll be back in a minute." He then crawled into the inlet, grunting bestially.

I looked at the phone in my hand. If Josh never emerges from the pipe, I thought, I'll simply hit redial, explain the situation to his mom, and get the hell out of here. It doesn't get any cleaner than that.

As I was reveling in the convenience of the scenario, Josh's voice shot from the pipe. "Meet me at the drainage ditch near I-15," he said, referring to an area of the drain we'd explored on the return trip.

"For what?" I asked him.

"Just meet me over there."

I struggled from the floor and backtracked to the ditch. A parallel tunnel appeared to be empty. No silhouette stood atop the embankments. I ducked back into the drain and waited for Josh.

"Matt!" I finally heard him call out.

I climbed out of the ditch and saw Josh—knife and headlamp in hand—leaning against a chain-link fence between Caesars Palace and I-15. Beads of sweat rioted on his forehead and he appeared to be having trouble breathing. "Are you OK?"

"Yeah," he said. "I just climbed out of that manhole over there." He pointed toward Bellagio, which stood proudly in the background. "The manhole cover was about a hundred pounds and hot as a frying pan," he continued. "I couldn't touch it with my hands. I had to use a shirt someone hung in the shaft to push the thing up."

My mind drifted. I imagined an aristocratic woman admiring the Strip from her $500-a-night suite atop Bellagio. Suddenly, a manhole cover pops open below. Josh—dressed in a wife-beater, Army pants, and muddy boots—squeezes out of the shaft. After retrieving his knife and headlamp from the smoldering asphalt, he limps toward the shade of a double-barrel drainage ditch. Would the woman gasp? Faint? How would she ever explain what she saw to her high-rolling husband?

"Give me a minute," said Josh, regaining control of his breathing. "I'm going to work my way around the fence. I think I saw a break a few hundred yards back."

Desperate for shade, I angled into the ditch and stood in the shadows of the storm drain. Finally, I began to understand why someone would live in the drains. They're ready-made reliable shanties—a floor, two walls, and a ceiling. They provide shelter from the intense Mojave heat and wind. (Remember, most desert animals live underground.) Some of the drains are dry for weeks, even months. And cops, security guards, and business owners don't dare roust anyone beyond the shade line.

But ultimately, the drains are deathtraps. They're disorienting and sometimes dangerously long. Many of them run under streets and contain pockets of carbon monoxide. They can be difficult to exit, particularly in a hurry. They're not patrolled. (Who would work *that* beat for $50,000 a year?) They're not monitored. There are no rules. There are no heroes. And, oh yeah, they can fill a foot per minute with floodwater.

Walking into a storm drain is like walking into a casino: You never know what's going to happen, but chances are it isn't going to be good.

ALL THE CONCRETE DREAMS IN MY MIND'S EYE

BY JOSHUA ELLIS

"When you got seven and all of a sudden it's twenty to seven, that means fourteen not thirteen."

The madwoman flailed against the barbwire fence, twisting her body back and forth, her eyes rolling at us. Matt was looking at her like she was a three-legged dog. She clutched her filthy Caesars Palace T-shirt.

"Yeah, yeah, yeah!" she said in rapid-fire ecstasy. "Render unto Caesar that which is Caesar's."

"And render unto God that which is God's," I finished.

The woman stared at me fearfully, then went back to muttering and swaying her body to and fro. I stared back. She was scrawny, red-faced, and sweating like a track star. Her hair was long, greasy. I couldn't tell if she was a schizophrenic, another Vegas meth freak, or both.

She was perched like a baleful crow between the fence and a ramshackle shed that sat behind a house in a downtown subdivision called the Biltmore Bungalows. I could only assume the name was some sort of cruel joke played on the residents, as none of the houses earned even bungalow status and this sure as hell wasn't the Biltmore Estate. It looked more like a place where cheap house paint goes to die, a place where middle-aged lunatics dance wildly on piles of rotting lumber.

Matt and I stood on the other side of the fence, attempting to ask the woman about the storm drain we'd just crawled out of. It lay 20 feet below us in a marshy ditch. It was the same drain Timmy "T.J." Weber told police he used to slip a dragnet after bashing his girlfriend's brains out and raping her 14-year-old daughter. We'd reversed his trail, arriving at this ditch where he entered the storm-drain system.

But the madwoman wasn't the ideal source. Her rolling eyes and disconnected narrative only added to the creepiness of the situation.

Matt and I'd accessed the drain behind Main Street Station (the same place I entered the system the first time I went underground). Three channels led in different directions. Freelance photographer Joel Lucas and I'd explored the northbound channel; the other two cradled ankle-deep water ... and I didn't really have the urge to feel slimy mud squishing in my boots for miles upon miles.

But I didn't have a choice this time around. Matt was determined to explore the tunnel Weber used to elude police. After all, he said, one of the main reasons we decided to explore the system was to find out what Weber had experienced—blinding darkness, shin-deep skank, and all.

But Matt and I *did* agree on one thing: We both wished that crazy bastard Weber had found a dry drain in which to play *The Fugitive.*

Soon after entering the channel that burrowed to the northeast, we realized this was the most surreal drain we'd explored all summer. The air reeked of decay and we could hear the constant churning of water somewhere in the distance. The walls and ceiling were covered with spider webs, two feet thick in areas. We felt like Frodo and Sam making their way through Shelob's lair. I half-expected to come across a half-eaten corpse tangled in the webs, the grisly remains of some poor bastard who'd stumbled down here by accident and been ambushed by whatever horrible arachnid created this tableau.

For the first time all summer, Matt and I began to freak out. We moved much more quickly than usual, as there was no one to interview in this narrow hell. No one had been in this tunnel for years—except Weber. I imagined him stumbling through the darkness, hands covered in blood, listening above the roaring water for the barking of police dogs.

Matt and I passed several lateral pipes, some big enough to walk in and each spitting water into the main tunnel. As we approached the pipes, I held my knife out in case something leapt at us. I wasn't sure what might be there, exactly, but I wasn't taking any chances.

Finally, the floor became corrugated and the tunnel began to roll down-hill. We eased down the slippery washboard surface, toward the light. Splashing into the ditch, we exhaled and knocked the cobwebs off our clothes. Like Frodo and Sam, we were happy to have made it out of the lair—but we weren't out of danger.

After briefly exploring a downstream drain, we climbed some rungs to the top of the south bank. And that's where we encountered the madwoman.

"ITT Technical Institute," said the woman, apropos of nothing. "It's an electrical dilemma. A root, a fruit, a gay man."

She glared at me. "Let me see the back of your shirt. I'll hold out my hand and see if I can read it."

I turned around and let her study my Dr. Martens tee. "Oh my God!" she said in horror. "That's what I thought." The woman clasped her hands together, stared at the horizon, and fell silent, as if expecting someone or something to swoop down from the heavens and carry her away.

"Do you know anything about the tunnels down there?" Matt asked the woman.

Her eyes rolled toward him. "A lot of crap has been going on down there the past few days," she said. "You might want to look in there. I feel really jumpy, the road gets bumpy."

"Thanks," said Matt, giving up on the interview. "Take it easy."

Matt and I backed away from the fence and turned around, eyeing an unlocked gate on the other side of the ditch. To get to the gate, we had to tightrope-walk the top of the south bank and use the fence for balance. Matt started out onto the narrow ledge. I followed him. Rabid dogs crashed against the chain links, nipping at our heels. The madwoman continued to mutter and sway to the rhythm of the urban runoff, atop the pile of rotting lumber.

"Ask Don Henley," she said, as Matt and I balanced high above the ditch. "This is the end of the innocence."

ONE CAN FIND SO MANY PAINS WHEN THE RAIN IS FALLING

The sky was a thousand shades of blue and the street a slick black. Raindrops bounced off the windshield of my Camry, headed west on Desert Inn Road. The wipers screeched loudly. Josh sat quietly in the passenger seat, adjusting the strap of his headlamp, dressed in a long-sleeve black T-shirt, black jeans, and black work boots. Fiddling with the radio tuner, I was wearing a long-sleeve black tee, Army-green cargo pants, and combat boots. "A Hard Rain's A-Gonna Fall" broke the silence:

"AND WHAT DID YOU HEAR, MY BLUE-EYED SON?
AND WHAT DID YOU HEAR, MY DARLING YOUNG ONE?
I HEARD THE SOUND OF A THUNDER, IT ROARED OUT A WARNING,
HEARD THE ROAR OF A WAVE THAT COULD DROWN THE WHOLE WORLD."

We crossed Paradise Road, then cut under the Strip at 50 miles per hour. The radio went dead … and then came back to life. An assortment of gear shifted around in the back seat. At Valley View Boulevard, I flipped a bitch and found my way onto Industrial. Warehouses, strip malls, and adult bookstores blurred by the windows. Finally, I pulled into the parking lot of a business complex north of the Flamingo Wash.

The air reeked of rain. Though I'd parked more than 200 feet from the wash in an attempt to be discreet, Josh and I could hear and feel its rumble. Josh gathered his gear from the back seat, then disappeared into the dusk. He returned shortly with a demented smile.

"Oh shit, man," he said. "The wash is flooded."

"How bad is it?" I asked, fitting the hard hat onto my head.

"Pretty bad."

I scooped the flashlight and golf club from the back seat, then jogged to the north bank. Rivulets ran down the near side of the wash and the far side cradled a chocolate-milk-colored stream, which tumbled toward the six-tunnel storm drain. I glanced at the sky. It was a medley of thunderclouds, smoke from wildfires to the west, and looming darkness. Before I could protest, Josh angled into the wash and started for one of the middle tunnels.

"Let's go in the south tunnel," I said. "That's where the Asian guy was."

During our virgin exploration of the drain, Josh and I stumbled on an Asian man about 300 feet into the tunnel. He lay motionless on two wooden pallets, which were supported by steel poles that stretched across the tunnel and rested on catwalks. Initially, I thought the man was dead—another victim of heat exhaustion, a heart attack, or a suicide-drug overdose; his skin was pale and he didn't respond to a series of questions. But he finally opened his eyes, as if waking from a 20-year sleep, and stared up at us blindly.

"Are you OK?" I asked the man.

He answered in a language that I assumed was Chinese.

"Is there anything I can do for you?"

The man mumbled another response that I couldn't interpret. Assuming that he didn't speak English and he wasn't in any danger, Josh and I continued on our way. But now, as we watched the floodwater funnel into the south tunnel, we were seriously concerned about his well-being.

Josh and I waded warily into the tunnel. The water was knee-deep and moving 15 miles per hour. "This is fucking frightening!" I said into the tape recorder dangling from my neck. "I can't believe we're doing this!" We climbed onto one of the catwalks, which was littered with matchbooks and cigarette butts. We stepped over plastic bags filled with trash. And then we reached the Asian man's makeshift bed, which stretched over the water like a bridge over the Amazon. It was empty.

Unsure if the man had found refuge from the storm or been washed away, Josh and I continued into the drain. Our boots thrashed through the water, creating the sound of a herd of horses crossing a shallow river.

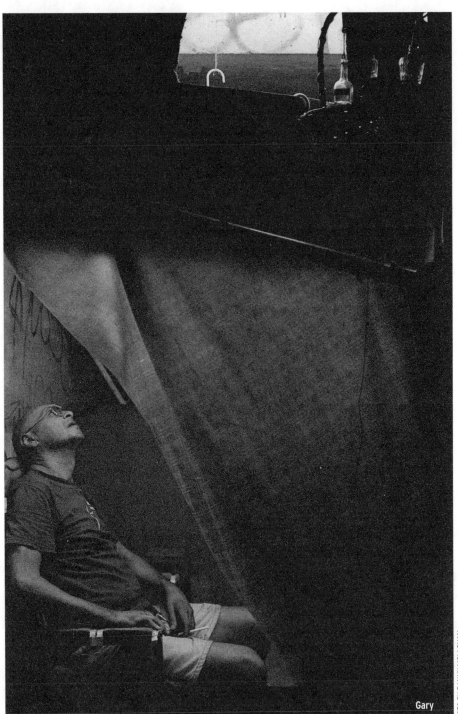

Gary

The art gallery, so glorious during the day, possessed an evil appearance. The lateral pipe Josh explored dumped water into the chamber, creating eddies and a formidable crosscurrent. Using the golf club as a plumb bob, we waded about the gallery. The beams of our flashlights awakened the graffiti ghosts.

Spellbound and scared, Josh and I turned into one of the middle tunnels and started back toward the inlet. We wanted to check on Gary. We'd discovered Gary's camp (a stool, cooler, and cardboard hut) during our first exploration of the drain and we talked to him a few days later. He told us that he'd moved from Seattle to Las Vegas 20 years ago to kick a cocaine habit—making him, as far as Josh and I could tell, the only person to come to Vegas to get *away* from drugs. While leaving the coke behind, said Gary, he found plenty of meth-amphetamine in Vegas. (Doesn't everybody?) Laziness and a meth addiction have kept him on the streets, he said. He has lived in the drain for about a year.

Walking upstream in floodwater, Josh and I discovered, was much more difficult than walking downstream. The water went af-ter our legs like a linebacker in the final year of his contract. Rocks, pine cones, beer bottles, spray-paint cans, and four-by-fours slammed against our shins, and our feet felt as heavy as cinderblocks. With dif-ficulty, we climbed a sandbar. As we splashed down into a knee-deep pool, a beam of light shot from the darkness.

"Gary?" I said, shielding my eyes with my free hand. "It's Matt and Josh."

"Hey, guys," said Gary dejectedly, taking the beam off us and sweeping it over his camp. The stool stood in three inches of water, the cooler threatened to float away, and the bottom of the hut was wet and collapsing.

"We came down here to check on you," said Josh. "Are you all right?"

"Yeah," said Gary, wearing cutoff shorts and sneakers. A T-shirt was tucked into the small of his back. "I was in the Stardust's sports book. I came back down here to see if anything had washed away."

"Is everything still here?" I asked him, surveying the camp. It looked more like scattered debris, the random dregs of a flood, than somebody's home.

"Yeah. I think so."

"What are you going to do?" asked Josh.

"I don't know," said Gary, scratching his bald head. He was tan, clean-shaven, and shiny. He looked a little like Mr. Clean ... with a 20-year meth addiction. "I used to have a few friends who lived in a house not too far from here, but they moved out. I used to stay with them when it rained. But now I don't know what I'm going to do."

"You should get a motel room," I said, reaching into my back pocket. "It's raining now and it looks like more's on the way. Don't even risk it, man."

I gave Gary all the money I had on me, which was only $12. (I'd taken it into the drain for bargaining purposes, in case things got *real* ugly.) Josh gave him seven or eight bucks.

"That's all I have on me," said Josh, shrugging. "It'll help you get a motel room. You don't want to stay down here tonight, man. It's way too dangerous."

Gary thanked us for the cash, then stuffed it into a pocket. Josh and I turned around and started downstream.

"Hey," I said over my shoulder. "Do you know if the Asian guy's OK?"

"No," said Gary. "I haven't seen him in a while. The last time I saw him was when the cops came down here. That was right after the whole T.J. Weber thing. They took us outside and questioned us. The Asian guy had an outstanding warrant, so they arrested him. He had a big wad of money on him, too. I have no idea how he got it."

"Does he speak any English?"

"I don't think so. I really don't know much about the guy."

"OK, man," I said. "Take care."

"OK," said Gary. "You, too."

Josh and I splashed through the pool and climbed the sandbar. We waded through the art gallery and pulled up at the mouth of the south tunnel—30 feet wide, eight feet high, and roaring like a jet engine at takeoff. We realized that if we were going to turn around, this was the place to do it. Underneath the Strip, the drain didn't have any manholes or lateral tunnels or even a proper niche. If a wall of water crept up behind us, our only hope would be to somehow ride the wave and grab onto something—anything ... a rung, a column, the leg of an unsuspecting tourist—on the other side of the Strip.

Josh and I looked at each other, smiled, then splashed into the tunnel.

The floodwater climbed halfway up the golf club and visibility was a cruel and lame joke. The air was so dark and heavy and foul that I could barely see Josh, who was walking right beside me. Initially, the floor was rocky and slick. But it soon smoothed out and footing became a secondary concern. Our main concern was the wires that sprung from the junction boxes on the ceiling and coiled into the water like electric snakes.

Josh and I had neither the time nor inclination to try to explain what we were seeing—the light fixtures, power outlets, and water pipes that ran along the ceiling. We were simply trying to survive. We ducked under a rainbow of runoff that poured from a lateral pipe and we weaved around concrete columns, half-expecting to find the Asian man's body tangled among the debris. The walls seemed to be shaking. Are we in a storm drain, I wondered, or an automated carwash stuck on the most expensive and violent setting? I kept waiting for one of those furry rotating brushes to come rolling out of the dark.

Suddenly, the tape recorder jumped off the snap hook and splashed into the stream. It went under, recording lights blazing like the eyes of a piranha.

"Goddammit!" I screamed. "I just lost the tape recorder."

"You're shitting me," said Josh.

"It had all my notes on it—not that I'll ever forget what I've seen and heard tonight."

"Did it have any other interviews on it?"

"No. But it was a Sony, man. The fucking thing cost sixty bucks."

If Josh and I'd found the recorder nestled in a pile of debris, lights blazing, it would've made one hell of a Sony commercial. But the endorsement contracts were not to be. We splashed under Caesars

Palace, the Strip, and the Imperial Palace without being jumped by a wall of water ... without discovering the Asian man's body ... and without finding the recorder.

We weaved through the columns and approached the IP's driveway. The entire sectioned wall was held open by chains. An elderly couple stood on the edge of the driveway, watching the water rush from the chamber and turn downstream. They didn't seem at all startled when Josh and I emerged from the darkness, drenched in runoff and sweat. It was as if they'd seen this kind of shit all week long in Vegas.

"Are you staying at the Imperial Palace?" I asked the couple, removing the hard hat and wiping my brow with my sleeve.

"Yes, we are," said the man.

"Did you have any idea its driveway was a flood channel?"

"No, we didn't," said the woman, disconcertedly.

"They didn't mention it when you checked in?"

"No."

"The Flamingo Wash starts on the west side of the Strip, cuts under Caesars Palace and the Imperial Palace, and empties right here," said Josh. "We just walked the entire length of the drain."

The couple remained unimpressed.

A security guard and a man in a suit were stationed on the edge of the driveway, like fishermen on a river bank. The suit—a pit boss, I assumed, who'd drawn the short straw to earn this shit shift—eyed me and Josh suspiciously.

"Well," I said to the couple, "enjoy your stay."

Josh and I started up the driveway. Reaching the Strip, we turned south on a sidewalk. The rain had stopped and a herd of tourists stampeded us, carrying cell phones and shopping bags, camcorders perched on their shoulders like rocket launchers. We angled over to the edge of the sidewalk, where a man in a hat and headphones handed us fliers: "One Girl for $35, Two Girls for $80, or Three Girls for $99." Well, I thought fleetingly, it *had* been a long day.

Josh and I crossed the street and continued south on the sidewalk. The promotions faded out and the squealing brakes of taxis, rental cars, and charter buses faded in. Arms jutted from passenger-side windows, aiming cameras and cell phones at the casinos. Awash in neon, Caesars Palace seemed as big and glorious as the Roman Empire in its heyday. We stopped in front of a fountain. Tourists posed prettily at the water's edge and fliers skimmed the surface. The storm drain—the Asian man's camp, the art gallery, and Gary—was somewhere below. I dug a penny out of my pocket, closed my eyes, and flipped it high in the sky.

Bill Shepherd, Marty Flynn, and Doug Drury

WASTEWATER WORLD

WHEN THE DOUBLE DOORS OPENED, the smell of 33.3 million gallons of raw sewage slapped me across the face. I gagged, then inched forward. In a dark and deep shaft decorated with spider webs, I could hear the rush of the sewage. It sounded like the Colorado River and smelled like the porta-potties at a redneck rock concert.

I craned my neck. In the semidarkness, about halfway down the 20-foot-deep shaft, I saw what appeared to be mechanical equipment and gears. Farther down, sunlight reflected off the brown wastewater.

"This is probably the most dramatic thing you'll see all day," said Doug Drury, deputy general manager of the Clark County Water Reclamation District.

On cue, Manager of Plant Operations Bill Shepherd threw a switch. The gears ground in the darkness and a 10-foot-long rake-like mechanism disappeared into the shaft. It reappeared wrapped in an assortment of wet debris, including toilet paper, tampons, Q-tips, paper towels, and cigarette butts.

Drury and Shepherd explained what was going on down there in the dark: Raw sewage from unincorporated Clark County was flowing into the plant in a main; the sewage filtered through a steel grate—or "bar screen"—which trapped debris; the rake-like mechanism scraped the debris off the grate and discarded it, allowing the sewage to flow freely and protecting equipment downstream.

The same thing was going on in two other shafts, they said.

"What are some of the stranger things the rake has brought up?" I asked.

Drury, Shepherd, and spokesman Marty Flynn laughed nervously and shook their heads. They then fell silent.

"Well," Shepherd finally said, "we've seen everything from car doors to bicycles to ..."

"Car doors and bicycles? How do they get in the system?"

"Construction connections are left open at times. Also, people will just open manhole covers and throw stuff down them. Anything they can get down a manhole they'll throw down a manhole. We've pulled palm trees out of manholes."

"We've found engine blocks," said Drury, noting there are more than 30,000 manholes in Clark County. "Just stuff put in there by vandals. They want to fill up the manholes with whatever they can find."

"And our least favorite," said Flynn, "fetuses. We've found a couple of those in the past several years."

My mind froze. I backed away from the shaft and squinted toward Flynn, who was blurred by the sunlight.

"How'd they get in the sewers?"

"We didn't see the medical reports, but our understanding was they were miscarriages that were accidentally flushed down the toilet."

A moment of silence. The rush of the sewage grew louder. I was five minutes into my tour of the Clark County Water Reclamation District's central sewage plant ... and I was already queasy. I'd already learned more than I ever wanted to about Las Vegas.

TWENTY YEARS AGO, DIRECTIONS TO the central sewage plant were simple: Take Flamingo Road east, cross Boulder Highway, then follow your nose. Indeed, the smell of the plant was stronger than anything emanating from Las Vegas City Hall or the Clark County Government Center.

But as the city sprawled, the plant began to practice "odor control." Now directions are more complicated: Take Flamingo east, cross Boulder Highway, pass a gantlet of gated communities, then follow *the signs.*

I followed these directions one morning in May 2006. It all started when I wrote a news brief about a U.S. Public Interest Research Group report titled "Troubled Waters." Using information provided by the Environmental Protection Agency, the report singled out sewage plants that violated the Clean Water Act between July 1, 2003, and December 31, 2004. The Laughlin Wastewater Reclamation Facility, run by the Reclamation District, was included in the report.

According to "Troubled Waters," the Laughlin plant—which empties into the Colorado River—wasn't up to standards in four of the five quarters between October 2002 and December 2003. It exceeded its phosphorus levels by 38%, its chlorine levels by 40%, and its ammonia levels by 89%.

I called Flynn to get the Reclamation District's side of the story. He helped me arrange an interview with Drury, who said the violations were related to maintenance problems that have since been fixed, then invited me to the central plant.

"While a trip to the 'Poop Plant' isn't high on most people's must-see list," said Flynn, who's worked at the plant 25 years, "we've found that our local media contacts have been able to write about wastewater treatment much more knowledgeably after seeing for themselves what it's all about."

I hesitated. Could the trip lead to a story? Do I really *want* to know how sewage is treated? Could I catch cholera, dysentery, or typhoid fever?

Finally, I took Flynn up on his offer. I'd explored trailer parks, weekly motels, no-cover-charge strip joints, and storm drains. Why not explore a sewage plant? Maybe it *would* lead to a story. Maybe I'd have fun out there in all the muck, grit, and stink. Maybe I'd learn something about Las Vegas.

I didn't have anything to lose, I decided—except my lunch.

Drury, Shepherd, and Flynn met me in the plant's lobby, which was sleek and modern. This may not be so bad after all, I thought, admiring the stylish architecture. It's the Taj Mahal of sewage plants. It's Bellagio ... without slot machines and tourists.

The way they were dressed—button-down shirts, slacks, and loafers—made me feel even more comfortable. Are we touring a sewage plant or the governor's mansion? This will be cake.

But before the flowery scent of the lobby could seep into my clothes—a secondhand shirt, cargo pants, and Chuck Taylors—I was hustled out the back door and into a golf cart, then driven to the gated area of the plant. Our first stop was the bar screen. (I guess Flynn likes to freak out his "local media contacts.") Our second was the grit-removal building, where we climbed some stairs and entered a room cluttered with platforms, catwalks, and pipes. The smell was overwhelming.

"Yum, yum, yum," said Flynn. "Is it lunchtime yet?"

"Almost," said Shepherd, who's also worked at the plant 25 years, licking his lips. These guys definitely had their act down.

I followed Shepherd, who's five-foot-four with spiky salt-and-pepper hair and a goatee, across the main platform to a railing. Chutes churned overhead, dropping black grit into dump trucks. Plastic bags, rubber gloves, and shriveled-up condoms dotted the grit.

Leaning over the railing, credentials swinging from his neck, Shepherd explained what we were seeing: Debris that slips through the bar screens settles in the sewage and is pumped out; it's processed, then deposited in the chutes; the trucks transport it (and the bar-screenings, which are washed and compacted in a downstairs room) to a landfill.

Twelve to 16 tons of grit and screenings a week are trucked from the plant.

"Periodically, we'll find money in there," said Shepherd, looking down at the grit.

"Who gets dibs on that?"

"Whoever finds it."

Flynn—six-foot-three, gray hair, clean-shaven—leaned against the railing. "If you get it," he said, "you can have it."

Drury and Shepherd laughed.

"You have to climb in the truck to get it?"

Plant workers use ladders to scale the side of the trucks and rake the grit to keep it level, said Shepherd.

"That's a full-time job? I mean, how's that listed on a ten-forty form?"

"Somebody's assigned to monitor this area and get the trucks filled up," said Shepherd, "and sometimes they have to knock the grit down."

"What's that pay?"

"They're part of my operations staff, and they have a lot of other duties, but it's not one of the glamour jobs out here."

Notebook in my left hand and pen in my right, I stared at the grit. My mind wandered and I thought about random things that could end up in the back of the trucks: bachelor-party condoms, dental floss discarded by a conventioneer, a hooker's lipstick-tinged cigarette butt, pills flushed down a toilet at the Hard Rock, strands of Wayne Newton's hair. Had a $100 bill ever found its way into the sewers and dropped from the chutes, I wondered? A $100 chip? A wedding ring?

"We've seen the bar screens and grit removal," said Shepherd, pulling me from my thoughts. "The next step is the primary clarifiers."

Primary clarifiers? They sounded like something I'd struggled with in my eighth-grade English class. Intrigued, I pushed off the railing and followed Drury, Shepherd, and Flynn across the platform, nostrils burning.

"On public tours, has anyone ever puked in this room?" I said, pinching my nose.

"We usually don't bring public tours in here," said Shepherd.

"If we get bratty kids on a tour," said Flynn, "we may bring them in here and lock the doors."

"Yeah," said Drury, five-foot-six with a paunch and gray-brown mustache. "You're getting the *special* tour."

"I'm flattered," I said, exiting the room and removing my hand from my nose.

DRURY, SHEPHERD, FLYNN, AND I climbed into the cart and drove deeper into the plant. Control panels, three-foot-diameter pipes, hieroglyphic letters and numbers—everything looked foreign. I felt like Marlow, the narrator of Conrad's *Heart of Darkness*, venturing into the jungles of the Congo. I kept waiting for natives to emerge from behind a windowless building, faces painted and clutching spears.

To the north, pine trees shaded a cinder-block wall. Through the needles, I could see stucco facades and shiny windows and Spanish-tile roofs. My eyes fixed on the familiar sight.

"Those people don't mind living next to a sewage plant?" I asked.

Flynn shifted in his seat. "They're aware of the plant when they buy their home," he said. "We try to do our best to contact them and communicate with them, but those are new homes. As the residents get settled in and start homeowners associations, we'll have direct communication with them. We want them to come and see the facility, understand what happens here, and be able to contact us if they have questions. We don't want to be a mystery."

"Do they ever complain about the smell?"

"Since those homes were built, we haven't had any complaints. I think part of it is the biofilters, which control the odor, have been operating really well. Years ago, they weren't a major component of the plant. Now, because we have neighbors, odor control is just as important as clean water."

We circled the grit-removal building and parked next to what appeared to be an aboveground pool. I flashed back to a job I had in college: I was a guinea pig for BioLab, an Atlanta-area company that makes pool chemicals. I stood in waist-high pools—relaxing, thinking, talking to my co-workers (Sharks and Minnows wasn't an option)—while lab-coated technicians dipped tubes in the water, testing how the chemicals reacted to humans and humans to the chemicals.

It wasn't a bad gig. I read a lot; it paid $20 an hour, which went a long way in the early '90s; and there weren't any long-term mental or physical effects (skin discoloration, depression, paranoia, impotence, a third leg).

But I didn't want to revisit the job, which was exactly what I was doing as Drury, Shepherd, Flynn, and I spilled out of the cart. I was, once again, standing in the test pool, leaning against its frying-pan-hot side, T-shirt wrapped around my head like a turban, checking out the cute female tech behind my mirrored sunglasses.

Approaching the pool-like shape, I snapped out of the flashback. I was not going to be climbing into that thing and wading around, regardless of hourly pay. It was ladder-less, 120 feet in diameter, and covered with a tarp. Shepherd lifted a flap, releasing a septic-tank smell and revealing brown water that was 12 feet deep.

Primary clarifiers, said Shepherd, hold the sewage for one and a half to two hours, allowing light solids to float to the top and heavy solids to sink to the bottom. The solids are skimmed off the top and scraped off the bottom, pumped out of the clarifiers, and processed as sludge. That, too, is trucked to the landfill.

"What would happen if I climbed in there?" I said, standing on my toes and squinting through the flap.

"You'd come out black and smelly and covered in grease," said Shepherd. "In these primaries, sludge sinks to the bottom and grease floats to the top. So if you happen to fall into one, you'd get a nice coat of grease all over you."

"You wouldn't get hurt?"

"No. There's a lot of bacteria in there, so you'd want to take a shower and flush out every orifice, but you'd survive."

"Has anyone ever fallen in one?"

"We've never had a person fall in one, but we had a mechanic jump in one once to get a tool he dropped."

"What?"

"He dropped his favorite tool and went in after it."

"Was he hurt?"

"No. We hustled him over to the shower and got him cleaned up, but that was about it."

"Is that part of the protocol out here? Jumping into primary clarifiers to get your tools?"

"It's not something we encourage. It was an impulse; he just wasn't thinking. All he knew was that he dropped his favorite tool, and he went in and got it."

"What kind of tool was it? It must've been valuable."

"I don't remember. It was so long ago. Shoot, that was probably twenty years ago. We haven't had anyone jump in recently."

I stared into the clarifier (and yes, it stared into me). The sewage was cloudy and I tried to think of something—anything—I'd follow into the abyss. My pen? Hah! My notebook? Strike two. My wallet? Not beneath the surface. A gold coin? Depends on its age, uniqueness, and condition. A showgirl? Depends on her age, uniqueness, and condition. A drowning child? I'd like to think so.

Drury interrupted my silly game. He said the bar screens, grit removal, and primary clarifiers are part of the physical (or primary) treatment process. The next step is biological (or secondary) treatment.

"This is where things *really* get interesting," he said.

WE WEAVED DEEPER INTO THE PLANT, deeper into the jungle. The cart was our boat. An asphalt path was our river. The motor purred like a leopard, but otherwise the plant was quiet and still. Suddenly, the smell of sewage ambushed us. Shepherd tapped the brakes, then parked next to a sprawling platform.

The platform, it turned out, included four "aeration basins." The basins were each 190 feet long, 100 feet wide, and 23 feet deep (a volume of 2.3 million gallons). They reminded me of Olympic-sized swimming pools—but cradled sewage, not chlorinated water.

In the basins, said Drury, bacteria latch onto solids in the sewage and help them settle. They also remove ammonia, phosphorus, and other contaminants. The aeration helps the bacteria grow. It also creates bubbles, which make the sewage look like a witches' brew.

"Champagne bubbles," said Drury, as we stood on the platform and stared down into one of the basins.

"That's not what I was thinking," I said, waiting for Kurtz to surface and breathe his last breath, "The horror! The horror!"

"You're seeing a thousand different species of bacteria in there.

In different sections of the basin, they do different things. We control the oxygen. We control the bacteria concentrations. We get different groups of bacteria to do different things in different sections. There's a lot going on in there."

Leaning over a railing, I could taste the sewage on my tongue. My skin began to itch. "How often do workers get sick out here?" I asked, backing away from the basin.

"Not very often," said Flynn. "They don't have contact with the sewage on a routine basis. Also, they wear goggles, face shields, and other protective gear. But basic hygiene is the most important safety precaution for someone working in this environment."

"Most people go into a restroom, use the bathroom, then wash their hands," said Shepherd. "If you work at a wastewater plant, you go into a restroom, wash your hands, use the bathroom, then wash your hands again. Personal hygiene is a habit you have to have when you work in this industry."

There was movement to the east. A sewage spill? A wild animal? Kurtz? I turned my head and saw a man approaching the platform on a three-wheel bicycle tricked out with chopper handlebars and chrome fenders. Assuming he was trespassing, I waited for Drury, Shepherd, or Flynn to order him off the property—but the man squeezed the brakes, lowered the kickstand, then climbed onto the platform. He had a goatee and was wearing shades. His uniform was baggy. Ladies and gentlemen: A. "Slick" Taylor, the coolest dude at the plant.

Taylor told me he started working at the plant part time in 1984, when he was 14 years old. He's now supervisor of operations. He manages a crew of specialists, technicians, operators, and trainees who monitor and maintain the plant and makes $81,500 a year.

"What's it like working here?" I asked him.

Taylor smiled. "Every day is different. At some jobs, you go in and do the same thing over and over again. In wastewater, it's not like that. Your day's dictated by how the plant's operating. A pump may go down. A valve may close. Something small can turn into something big real quick out here."

"How often do things go wrong?"

"Not often. And we've got enough experienced operators that when something does go wrong, we can usually take care of the problem."

"Is it gratifying work? Do you take pride in it?"

"I take pride in what we do, because it's for the environment. It's for me. It's for you. It's for everyone. We're the first and last defense before that water hits the Las Vegas Wash and then Lake Mead. If we don't treat the water, a lot of people are affected."

"How'd you end up working here?"

"There was a program that targeted youths in low-income areas of the Las Vegas Valley and gave them the opportunity to work summer jobs at places like this, the Water District, and Nevada Power," said Taylor, who was born and raised in Vegas. "I applied for the program and ended up here at the plant. I reapplied the next summer and came back again. I got to come back every year, and the more I came back, the more I learned. When it was time for me to put in for a permanent position, I was ready for it. I was seasoned, because the older operators had trained me."

"Any regrets about making this your career?"

"No regrets. The funny thing is, I remember when I got offered the operator position. My boss asked me what my plans were after high school. I said, 'Well, I got a couple basketball-scholarship offers I'm entertaining.' He said, 'You can go to college for four years, graduate, and not have a job. Or you can work here, start a career, and we'll pay you to go to school for wastewater treatment.' It wasn't a hard decision."

Taylor said he has taken classes at the Community College of Southern Nevada, but hasn't graduated.

"What's the best thing about working here?"

"The people. I work with a lot of good people. Over the years, you build relationships. We thrive on the team concept. We're all in it together. We understand that it's not about you or me or this or that. It's about treating that water."

"What are the people who work here like?"

"We have people from different ethnicities, different backgrounds. It's diverse, but we all get along pretty well. Every day is not going to be peaches and cream, but we make the best of it. We need each other. We rely on maintenance to make sure our pumps are working. We rely on the electrical guys to keep the power on. We all have to work together to get that water clean and out the back door."

"What's the worst thing about the job?"

"The worst thing is two experiences I've had. One time, a contractor was digging and he thought he was away from the main line coming into the plant. Well, he hit the line. Nothing but raw sewage was coming out of it. It was like the fire alarm went off. Everybody dropped everything. We were knee-deep in it, sandbagging and building a dam. I stunk for three days. It was horrible, but we had to get that water contained until we got the line fixed.

"The other time was Christmas of ninety-six or ninety-seven. Somehow we got our ratio off and we couldn't process the sludge; it wouldn't cake. For three days, we battled it: Imagine that hard cake being nothing but mush. It was blowing all over the place. That was one *bad* Christmas."

I turned toward the basin. "You ever seen anything strange in the sewage?"

"What do you mean by strange?"

"You know, weird stuff."

"Not in this part of the plant, but anything that can come down a sewer line can end up at the facility. The craziest thing I've seen at the bar screens is a bike. The bar screen actually picked the bike up, and when it dropped on the backside of the screen, it just hung there. We took a picture of it."

"I keep waiting for some strange beast to emerge from the water."

"Nah, man. The most interesting thing that can happen out here is if we have a pump malfunction or the aeration stops; the basin would be like a big sink with a bunch of suds. But the worst thing we've ever seen is a broken aerator."

"You think you'll retire out here?" I asked, turning toward Taylor.

A. "Slick" Taylor

"That's my plan. With the county, you can work till you're sixty-two or you can do thirty years and retire at any age. If everything goes right, I'll be able to retire at forty-nine. Will I leave at forty-nine? I don't know. I'll still be kind of young. We'll just have to wait and see."

"Will it be tough to leave after all these years?"

"Yeah, it'll be tough. I started my career here at a young age and I've been very fortunate. At retirement, I'll have spent more than fifty percent of my life at the plant, not including those five summers. I'll miss the people who mentored me. I'll miss the interaction with the team I work with. But the one thing I'll take with me is that I know I played an important part in ensuring the quality of the water leaving this plant."

Taylor and I shook hands and exchanged cards.

"What's the 'A' stand for?"

"Advergus."

"Is that a family name?"

"No. My godmother named me that. She found it unique and my mom let her name me."

"Why do they call you Slick?"

"Slick comes from one of the guys that retired from here, Glen Workman, a good friend of mine. My first summer, I think he was testing me to see what kind of worker I was. It was like the third week I was here and it was a hundred and eighteen outside. Back then for odor control, we used big fiberglass containers full of charcoal. We'd filter the bad air through the charcoal and out into the atmosphere. Over time, the charcoal starts breaking down and getting pushed to one side of the containers, so somebody has to go in there and put new charcoal down and spread it smooth.

"Well, Glen calls me on the radio and tells me to come to the control room. He says, 'You need to go into that container. Get a shovel, put on gloves, a mask, and a hood and start smoothing that charcoal out.' I said, 'OK, but I got to go to the bathroom first.' Well, I didn't go to the bathroom; I went and hid in the plant. It took him a good fifteen minutes to find me, but he finally did and said, 'Uh-huh.

You think you slick, but you can't get away from me.' And that's been my name ever since."

Drury, Shepherd, Flynn, Taylor, and I worked our way back to the path. Taylor pedaled into the sunlight, 50-spoke rims shining, and I followed Shepherd up some stairs, onto a catwalk, and over a secondary clarifier.

Like primary clarifiers, secondary clarifiers hold the sewage, allowing light solids to float to the top and heavy solids to sink to the bottom. Unlike primary clarifiers, they're not covered with a tarp. (The sewage doesn't smell as bad at this stage of the process.) I looked down. The clarifier was brown in the center, where the solids gathered, and green on the perimeter, where the water poured over a concrete rim and continued downstream.

THE CENTRAL SEWAGE PLANT—the first modern sewage plant in unincorporated Clark County—cost $3 million to build and opened in 1956, when the population of the county was 100,000. A few main lines pumped sewage to the 350-acre plant and it treated two million gallons a day. It had 189 customer accounts, including a handful of hotel-casinos on the Strip, and its only neighbor was a cattle and alfalfa farm.

"I recall hearing stories about how new guys at the plant would have cow duty," said Flynn, as our captain, Shepherd, steered us south. "They had to chase the cows out of the plant, because there was no fencing and nobody else around to do it.

"Another story I heard was about the way the police would deal with hookers back then. They'd pick them up, drive them out of town, and drop them off. By the time the hookers got back into town, they'd lost their business. This was one of the drop-off locations. Plant operators had these stories about how on Friday and Saturday nights, fashionably dressed women would drop by and ask to use the phone and if they could wait until their ride picked them up. That's how far removed the plant was from everything."

Today, the plant's worth more than $400 million. The population of the county is 1.9 million. More than 2,700 miles of pipeline

pump sewage to the 600-acre plant and it treats 100 million gallons a day. It has 175,000 customer accounts, including *all* the casinos on the Strip, and it's surrounded by homes, businesses, a horse park, golf course, and school.

Veering east, we got a glimpse of the plant's future. Four more aeration basins (rebar and wet concrete) were under construction. Men in hard hats and orange vests expanded a pump station. Five-foot-diameter pipes ran parallel to the path, waiting to be buried with the mobsters, prostitutes, stolen money, and other secrets of the Las Vegas desert.

Over the next five years, the Water Reclamation District plans to spend more than $493 million expanding and upgrading the plant.

Shepherd looked over his shoulder. Somewhere beneath the construction, he said, the sewage is being pumped through "dual media filters." The first filter is coal, he said. The second is sand.

"We've seen the bar screens, grit removal, primary clarifiers, aeration basins, secondary clarifiers, and filtration," said Shepherd, parking the cart in the shade of a mesquite. "The last thing we do is disinfect the water."

Drury, Flynn, and I followed Shepherd up some stairs, across a landing, and into a cinderblock building marked "5M." Shepherd opened two flaps in the floor, exposing a six-foot-wide and eight-foot-deep trench brimming with water. Ultraviolet light colored the water neon green.

"Most plants disinfect with chlorine," said Shepherd. "That used to be the standard, but we've gone to a process called 'ultraviolet disinfection.' We use a wavelength of ultraviolet light that's germicidal to the bacteria. The light, as it shines through the water, inactivates any organism and bacteria. It doesn't kill them, but it inactivates them so they can't reproduce. They only live a few hours, then die off."

Closing the flaps, Shepherd exited the building and walked to a concrete channel roaring with water. The water shimmered in the sunlight, then disappeared into a tunnel. According to control panels, 33.5 million gallons of treated sewage (or "effluent") were leaving the plant and its pH (acidity or alkalinity) was 6.8. The EPA's standard is between six and nine.

Shepherd dipped a plastic container into the water and held it to the sun. "How's it look?" he asked me.

"A little cloudy, but mostly clear."

He lowered the container. "Anything smell out of the ordinary?"

"It's a little musky, but not bad. Is it drinkable?"

"I wouldn't drink it," said Flynn, "but I'd swim in it."

"I practically live in Lake Mead," said Shepherd. "I love it. I'm a water nut. I'd swim in it without a problem. It meets those kind of standards, but it's not disinfected to drinking-water standards."

"We've had engineers visit us from other parts of the world," said Flynn. "Because the drinking-water standards in their countries aren't anywhere close to ours, they'll grab a sample out of here and drink it."

"Did they get sick?"

"No. It's cleaner than the water they drink at home."

I turned toward Shepherd. Away from the light, the water looked clean, as if it had poured from a faucet. I thought about reaching for the container, tipping it to my lips, and taking a swig; it would've been the ultimate test of the treatment process and a bold journalistic stroke. But I couldn't do it. Not after seeing the sewage seep through the bar screen. Not after smelling the grit-removal building. Not after tasting the witches' brew of the aeration basins. Not after hearing Slick's story about how the sludge wouldn't cake on Christmas. Not knowing that the bacteria were still alive.

THE LAST LEG OF OUR JOURNEY TOOK US off the plant's map: east on a two-lane road, through a break in a barbwire fence, and onto a concrete path (the roof of two twelve-by-four tunnels). Swinging south, the path was swallowed by a forest of tamarisk. If the tamarisk could be lifted like a curtain, I wondered, what would it reveal? Homeless camps? Illegal dumpsites? A kit fox stalking a rabbit?

A half-mile off the road, in the crossfire of quail calls, Shepherd

parked the cart in a clearing. Below, the tunnels emptied into a concrete channel. The effluent—three feet deep in areas—surged toward the Las Vegas Wash.

"Look at the size of that thing!" said Flynn, springing from the cart and standing on the north bank. "See it over there on the far side?"

A carp—hauntingly pale and 18 inches long—struggled against the current, with five of its ugliest friends. The freakish beasts would not have looked out of place in the Congo River.

"Do people fish down here?" I asked, sensing that we were being watched from the shrubs.

"I've never seen anyone fishing," said Flynn. "I've seen people building camps. I've seen people building meth labs. But no, not fishing."

Shepherd laughed. "One time, I had people from the Nevada EPA out here. We were taking a tour after a flood and we happened to look downstream. There was a lady sitting in a lounge chair in the middle of the wash, soaking her feet. Her husband was walking alongside the bank. Just as soon as I'd told the EPA that we never have people back here, there they were."

I followed Drury, Shepherd, and Flynn along the bank. Ducks zigzagged and buried their heads in the water. A handrail broke the surface at an angle. My mind drifted and I thought about the tour. I was glad I accepted Flynn's invitation. Three hours ago, when I entered the lobby, I knew very little about the plant, the people who work there, and the treatment process. Now, though dizzied by everything I saw, heard, and smelled, I felt initiated. I felt like part of the crew. In eight years of journalism, I couldn't remember learning more while researching a story. To know nothing about a subject and then, a few hours later, have a grasp of it—*that's* what I like most about my job, I realized as I walked the bank.

Images flashed though my mind: a fetus caught in the bar screen; a condom atop a pile of grit; Slick pedaling into the sunlight; a prostitute in a dress, hat, and gloves staggering out of the darkness and into the plant, high heels clicking on the asphalt; a tourist puking into a toilet and flushing, oblivious to where the wastewater goes, how it's treated, and who treats it.

"This is the epitome of something that's out of sight, out of mind," said Flynn. "You flush the toilet and you never think about where it's going, what happens to it, and who's taking care of it. You simply hope that somebody takes care of it. That's what we do. We take care of it, so nobody else has to worry about it."

"This goes into our main drinking-water source," said Shepherd, "but nobody ever thinks about that. Everybody comes here, parties, then goes home. They don't want to think about what happens to their waste products. But we do everything we can to produce quality water. There's a lot of pride taken in the effluent that leaves this plant. As the water flows into Lake Mead, we feel very good about what's coming back to us."

Reaching the confluence of the wash and channel, we squinted downstream. The water snaked to the southeast, then disappeared in the glare.

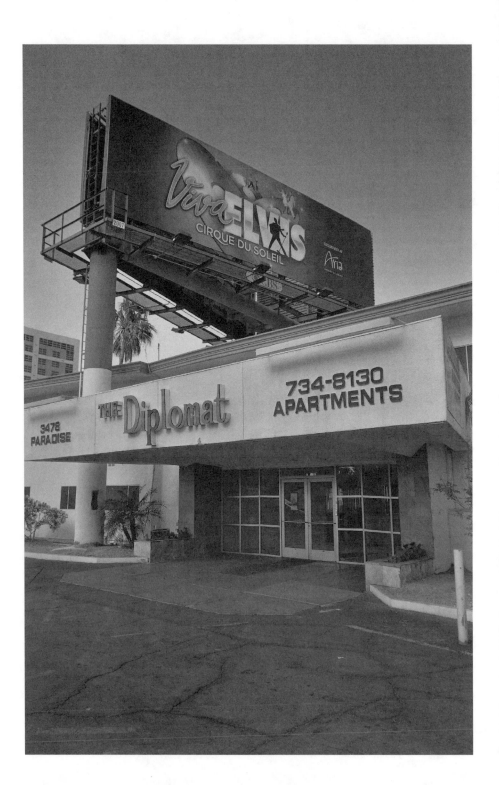

ANOTHER DAY ON PARADISE

IT WAS A SWATH OF DESERT A HALF-MILE EAST of the Strip, wedged between a trailer park and driving range. Power lines threaded the sky. Chain-link fences and cinder-block walls ("The Ridgecrest Boyz Wuz Here!") formed its border. It was littered with syringes, paper cups, plastic bags, and glass.

It was a no-man's land. Scorched earth. A real estate developer's worst nightmare. It was also, over the years, home to hundreds of people.

They lived in camps, from sheet tents to plywood mansions, camouflaged in the creosote and high grass. They cooked on makeshift grills. At night, they sat on cardboard mats, got high, and stared at the Strip—MGM Grand, Excalibur, Luxor, Mandalay Bay—and thought about getting off the junk, getting off the streets, and getting a job. Buzzed by planes taking off from McCarran International Airport, they thought about going home, reuniting with their families, maybe starting families of their own.

It was known as the "Field of Dreams."

For three years, I've had my own Field of Dreams. A half-mile east of the Strip. Bordered by chain-link fences and cinder-block walls ("Fuck the Pigz!"). At night, I stare at the Strip—the Wynn, Treasure Island, the Mirage, the Venetian—and think about writing a best-seller, moving into a downtown condo, and buying a new car. As the planes bank east and west, I think about going home to Atlanta, to San Francisco, to Europe.

The Diplomat apartments.

When my girlfriend and I broke up, I had to find a place to live—fast. My first choice was a two-bedroom condo for rent in a neighborhood east of UNLV, populated by coeds who ride retro bikes to class and read Neruda while sunbathing at the pool (or so I imagined). My backup was a loft at the Diplomat.

The Diplomat apartments sit on six and a half acres at the southeast corner of Paradise Road and Sierra Vista Drive, just south of Desert Inn Road. In the 1950s, Nevada Supreme Court justice Frank McNamee owned the land. In April 1959, he sold it to Wilbur Clark, frontman of the Desert Inn hotel-casino.

Clark hired Hugh E. Taylor (who designed the Desert Inn) to design the apartments, originally named the Palm House. The exterior took two days to draft, said Taylor, the interior a week.

"I went over to the Desert Inn one afternoon with the bill to see if Wilbur was around," said Taylor. "Sure enough, he was at a table with these other fellows. I went up to him when there was a break in the conversation and said, 'I have a bill here for the Palm House apartments. The plans are complete and have been delivered to the builder.' He had a cocktail in front of him and he just took the napkin out from under it, turned it over, and wrote 'Pay Bearer Ten Thousand Dollars.' Then he signed it and said, 'Take this to the casino cage.' I did and they counted out the money—no questions asked. I was amazed."

In December 1959, Clark sold the project to Wilton Construction Co. and the name of the apartments was changed. The Diplomat debuted in 1960, featuring a porte-cochere, football field-sized courtyard, and bow tie-shaped pool. (The building and lobby are also shaped like a bow tie.) It had 70 units—20 one-bedroom, 40 two-bedroom, 10 three-bedroom—all draped, carpeted, and fully furnished. One-bedroom apartments started at $200, two-bedroom $275, and three-bedroom $325 (including utilities).

Behind the DI and within a mile of the Riviera, Stardust, Thunderbird, and Sahara, the Diplomat was home to actors, showgirls, mobsters, magicians, casino executives, comedians, lounge singers, and showroom stars. Judy Garland lived in apartment 125, according to property managers Jan and O.J. Hasner. (The apartment features decorative doors, custom shelves, and a 10-foot-wide and three-foot-high living-room mirror.) Betty Grable lived in 132, said fan and friend Bob Isoz. Dean Martin in 139. Ann-Margret and Louis Prima also lived at the complex.

"It was completely charming," said Isoz, who's lived at the Diplomat since 1992. "It was also private and secluded, yet close to the Strip and everything else. The stars that stayed here didn't have parking spaces; their limousines pulled up alongside the building and they went in the back door. That's why a lot of the apartments have beautiful walk-in closets; they were used to store the costumes of the stars that lived here."

When I moved in, the Diplomat—like many Las Vegas headliners—was past its prime. The stucco and wood-frame building was dingy, its trim faded. There were no showgirls (or coeds) by the pool. It was home to cabbies, construction workers, card dealers, bartenders, truckers, front-desk clerks, punk rockers, and retirees.

I found a crack pipe (not a headdress or sequined jacket) in the closet.

There were 177 units—101 one-bedroom, 54 two-bedroom, four three-bedroom, 18 lofts—all unfurnished. One-bedroom apartments started at $500, two-bedroom $875, three-bedroom $1,075, and lofts $725 (including utilities).

"The first day I walked the property, I came around the side of the building and saw a really good-looking woman digging around in the dumpster," said O.J. Hasner, who's managed the apartments with his wife since 2003. "I'm thinking, 'What's going on here? Could she be a tenant that lost something?' I get a little closer and she turns around and looks at me and laughs—and it was straight out of a mental institution. I was like, 'Wow, now I know why you're digging around in there. Somebody let you out of an institution and turned you loose on the streets.' She was straight-up crazy. She was beautiful, but nuttier than a fruitcake."

Valentino Santiago

The neighborhood—bordered by Paradise, Desert Inn, Maryland Parkway, and Flamingo Road—had also deteriorated. Called the "most desirable apartment area in Las Vegas" in a 1963 business proposal, it was deemed the "worst neighborhood in the city" by the *Las Vegas Weekly* in 2005. Residents nicknamed it "Crack Alley" and the "Ho Stroll." Caution tape decorated the parking lots, sidewalks, and streets.

"This wouldn't be my first choice of places to live," said Metro lieutenant Jack Owen, who's worked the beat off and on for 10 years. "There's a lot going on here."

In 2005, 11 murders, 40 sexual assaults, 184 robberies, 275 burglaries, 288 car burglaries, and 477 car thefts were reported in the area.

I knew the neighborhood was rough—I lived on its north border for three and a half years—but I was drawn to the Diplomat. It was central and between two of my favorite areas, downtown and UNLV. The courtyard was green and shaded by palm, olive, and mulberry trees. Featuring cathedral ceilings, hidden staircases, and lofted bedrooms, the floor plans were unique. And the price was right.

I signed a six-month lease, figuring that would give me time to get over my ex-girlfriend, save some money, and find a more permanent place to live. Three years later, I'm still here (and I'm not planning to move anytime soon).

My friends thought I was crazy to live at the Diplomat—and I had my own concerns—but I became more and more comfortable with the complex. It's convenient; I can walk to the Strip and to bars, restaurants, and coffee shops on Paradise. It's safe and well-maintained. The residents are friendly and eccentric.

My next-door neighbor Valentino Santiago is a stylist and fashion designer who's worked for *Jubilee!*, *Siegfried & Roy*, and Celine Dion's *A New Day*. Born in Philadelphia and raised in the Bronx, he's lived at the Diplomat since 1996.

"I don't know who lived in my apartment before me, but I'm dying to find out if they were famous," said Santiago, whose loft is cluttered with vases, sculptures, mannequins, Renaissance paintings, suits of armor, and sewing machines. "I believe in my heart they were famous, because so many celebrities lived here and this apartment has such great energy. Maybe Desi Arnaz or Lucille Ball lived here. Maybe Dean Martin. Maybe Siegfried and Roy. I don't know, but I do know the Diplomat's been a blessing to me. I have a lot of beautiful memories here. It's come to mean home."

My other next-door neighbor, Don Tate, dealt craps for 14 years at the Gold Coast, the Golden Gate, and Casino Royale and was a pit boss for 11 years at Casino Royale. A cancer survivor (diagnosed with non-Hodgkin's lymphoma in 2000, he was told he had eight months to live), he works from home as a studio engineer. He's lived at the Diplomat since 2003.

"This is where I beat cancer," said Tate, whose loft is cluttered with amps, mixers, guitars, keyboards, monitors, and drum machines. "Living here gave me a purpose, a sense of self. I was getting ready to go into my fourth round of chemo and was living with a co-worker who was helping me out, but he was moving. I moved in here and right after that I found out about stem-cell research and got accepted into the Nevada Cancer Institute. I lived. That's what I'll remember most about this place."

I also became more comfortable with the neighborhood. Though old, crowded, and crumbling, it's not as hellish as the headlines and statistics suggest. Most of the crimes are committed on four or five blocks, which I avoid at night. Since 2005, because Metro has focused on the area, murders, sexual assaults, car burglaries, and car thefts have decreased. Prostitutes stand under streetlights and drug dealers make eye contact with motorists—but most of the residents are law-abiding and hardworking and just trying to survive ... and one layoff, injury, or addiction away from the streets.

In 2006, a developer bought the Field of Dreams (parcel 162-21-810-015) and it was cleared and fenced. A timeshare now occupies the land. When will a developer buy the Diplomat, my neighbors and I wonder? When will it be cleared and fenced? When will a timeshare, hotel-casino, or high-rise condo occupy the land?

Not anytime soon, said Sean Hay of Emser International, which has owned the Diplomat since 1991. But my neighbors and I are leery. We've seen too many apartment complexes in the neighborhood sold to developers or the Las Vegas Convention Center ... and boarded up, wrapped in caution tape, and bulldozed.

They keep paving Paradise (and Sierra Vista) and putting up parking lots.

"When they tear this place down, which could happen any day now, I don't know where I'll go," said Phyllis Watson, a retired office clerk who's lived at the Diplomat since 1987. "I won't find anyplace cheaper than this in town. I may move to St. George, Utah; I have a friend there. I may move to Iowa, where my brother and sister live, but it's so cold.

"I don't know. I guess I'll just sit here until they tell me they're going to tear it down and then figure it out from there."

I'll do the same. Then I'll pack up my books, laptop, and steno pads full of thoughts and move on to the next place:

Standing in the courtyard of the Diplomat, I close my eyes and try to picture the complex 45 years ago. The building is bright white, its trim rich brown. Showgirls—topless and stretched on chaise lounges—surround the pool, Dino the only man among them. Judy Garland stares blankly out the window of apartment 125, stirring vodka into a glass of orange juice with her finger.

.　.　.

In the summer, cicadas—ignoring Aesop's advice—sing in the courtyard trees. In the winter, the courtyard is quiet and dry shells cling to the bark.

Standing on my patio staring at the shells, I think about all the people who've shed their skin in L.A., San Francisco, New York, Chicago, Detroit, Dallas, Cleveland, and Kansas City, flown away, and landed in Las Vegas. How many of them lived at the Diplomat? How many of them lived in my apartment? Did they ever find what they were looking for?

.　.　.

One of the conveniences of living at the Diplomat is you don't have to carry donations to your car and drive to Goodwill or the Salvation Army. You simply set them next to the dumpster and—voila!—they vanish. Eliminate the middleman.

Once an hour, a dumpster diver, scrapper, pawner, or scavenger of some sort approaches the trash bin. They arrive on foot, bike, or in a truck. They push grocery carts ... garbage bags are slung over their shoulder as they pedal ... or they spill out of the flatbed like the Joad family. In the summer, they throw a towel or blanket over the front of the bin, so they don't get burned. In the winter, the bin's as cold as the barrel of a gun.

I've seen my neighbors digging through the dumpster. (Later, they asked me if I wanted to buy a Rolodex or some CDs.) I've seen a woman pushing a stroller stick her nose in the bin. I've seen a man in a wheelchair use the arm slot to help him stand, raise his harpoon high like Captain Ahab, and spear an aluminum fish.

. . .

When I woke this morning, I got your message. You said I can't write. You said I can't fuck. You said I'll always be alone.

I can be ... the river card you need ... the leaves crunching beneath your feet ... the only tree standing after a forest fire ...

But, sweetheart, you have to call before midnight.

. . .

I said, you amaze me. You said, you inspire me. I said, there's no place I'd rather be than playing pool with you in a dive bar, drinking dollar drafts, and making out between shots. You said, I'm hustling you. I said, I'd never let numbers on a birth certificate tell me who I can love. You said, I've never been good with math anyway. I said, you're sweet and smart and crazy and divine. You said, I'm buzzed and confused and intimidated and happy.

I meant everything I said, love. And when I slipped my jacket over your shoulders that early morning in December, I hoped to get it back.

. . .

Mark Conway and Erica Williams, Diplomat residents since 2003

It's one twenty-two a.m. and I'm as lonely as Macbeth in his castle. Cats tiptoe across the roof. A faucet drips. How can an apartment so close to the Strip and Paradise Road be so quiet?

I surfed the Net, read a chapter of a book, and watched a movie, but I can't fall asleep. Tonight, the silence is too loud. I splash water on my face and throw on a T-shirt, cargo pants, and sneakers. Downstairs at the bar, I stuff my driver's license and $10 (coffee and dessert) into one back pocket and my notepad into the other. I exit the apartment and start south on Paradise.

The Strip struts across the horizon. Exhaust fumes foul the air. Above the rush of traffic, I hear the click-click-click of the monorail.

As panhandlers raise their Starbucks cups, prostitutes pirouette on the street corners, and credit hustlers weave in and out of the casinos, I reach for the notepad.

. . .

At least once a month, I see someone walking through the neighborhood carrying electronic equipment: a TV, VCR, DVD recorder, computer monitor. Maybe they stole the equipment and plan to pawn it or sell it on the street for drug money. But I like to think their addiction to technology has hit rock bottom and they're destined for the nearest dumpster.

. . .

Sneakers swing from the power lines above Sierra Vista, Swenson Street, and Cambridge Street. Maybe they mark gang turf or a crack house. But I like to think they're left behind by the young men murdered on the streets, as they begin their journey to immortality.

. . .

In 2007, eight murders, 37 sexual assaults, 197 robberies, 322 burglaries, 146 car burglaries, and 264 car thefts were reported in the area. The number of times I was victimized by a crime: 0.

. . .

Strange sight of the day: a man standing on the corner of Sierra Vista and Swenson with his shirt tied around his waist and his pants draped over his shoulders, caution tape strung through the belt loops.

. . .

Move-in specials. Cobweb dreamcatchers. Paper-clip zippers. Drained pools. Stray cats. Kamikaze pigeons. Flight patterns. Flood channels. Power stations. Foreclosed dreams. Cardboard condos. Madman monologues. Street prophets. Street profits. Razor-blade alleys. Guillotine sunsets. Junkyard angels. Coyote smiles. Barbwire bracelets. Pawnshop wedding rings. Heart-shaped bruises. Glass mosaics. Chicken-bone sculptures. Employees of the month. Sandcastles. Plastic cities.

. . .

T-shirt design for locals living near the Strip: art on the front—a camera crossed out by a "no" symbol; text on the back—"No, I Won't Take Your Fucking Picture!"

. . .

It's hard to describe what it feels like to be cruising south on the Strip and to be passed by your landlords, who are tattooed ("Death Before Dishonor"), straddling a Harley, and draped in leather. Note to self: Pay the rent on time!

. . .

The pyramids of Egypt were built to help pharaohs reach the Milky Way, the Nile of the sky. Luxor was built to help drag middle-class Midwesterners into the gutter.

. . .

They buy a one-way ticket to Vegas, park their rental car in the Stratosphere's garage, and stuff a note into their pocket: "There are no answers." They leave the car keys at the front desk, pose for a souvenir photo, and take the elevator to the 109th floor. Lightheaded, they spin through the revolving door and spill onto the observation deck. It's not as cold or windy as they expected. What a beautiful day to die!

They climb the guard rails, balance on the ledge, and survey the valley: mountains, Spanish-tile roofs, golf courses, McCarran airport, the Strip. They're surprised there are so many trees. They're surprised, 1,000 feet above Las Vegas Boulevard, they can hear sirens and see people standing on street corners and distinguish the make and model of cars.

The city looks even less real from up here, they think.

When the security guard arrives, out of breath, they're gone. Tourists on the deck are looking down, wide-eyed, hands covering their mouths—and those on the thrill rides are screaming.

. . .

All those dancing lights. All those dead-end dreams. All those opened hands. All those closed minds. All those cardboard hearts. All those rattlesnake handshakes. All those sad-eyed dealers. All those busted cards. All those tumbleweed dice. All those gasoline drinks. All those bus-stop women. All those suicide motel rooms. All those holocaust days. All those Shackleton nights. All those Pearl Harbor sunrises.

This city takes so much ... and gives so little.

· · ·

Vegas rule 284: If you circled job ads in the classified section of the morning paper, don't circle football bets in the sports section.

· · ·

I watched *The Truman Show* last night and woke this morning wondering if my life, like Truman Burbank's, is a reality TV show. Is Las Vegas, like Seahaven, a domed studio? Are my friends actors? Is every action—a come-out roll at three-thirty a.m. in a downtown casino—choreographed by a director?

If so, that would explain a lot.

Rolling over in bed, I imagine realizing something is wrong and wanting to escape the city. I climb into my car and—despite traffic jams, a flat tire, and a dust storm—access a mountain road. Suddenly, I crash into the studio wall. I spill out of the car, stagger up some stairs, and open an exit door.

"Matt."

I turn around. No one's there.

"You can speak," says a voice from above. "I can hear you."

"Who are you?" I ask.

"I'm the creator of a television show that gives hope and joy and inspiration to millions."

"Then who am I?"

"You're the star."

I pause. "Was nothing real?"

"You were real. That's what made you so good to watch."

I drop my head and turn toward the exit.

"Listen to me, Matt. There's no more truth out there than in the world I created for you. Same lies. Same deceit. But in my world you

Jan and O.J. Hasner

have nothing to fear. I know you better than you know yourself."

I stop.

"You're afraid. That's why you can't leave. It's OK, Matt. I understand. You belong here with me. Talk to me. Say something. Say something, goddammit! You're on television! You're live to the whole world!"

I turn around and stare into the camera. "In case I don't see you: Good afternoon, good evening, and good night!"

I bow, then exit into a black void.

. . .

Vegas rule 327: These friends have wings, they won't stay long.

. . .

Jan Hasner said former tenants visit the Diplomat to walk the courtyard and reminisce. What do they think about, I wonder? An addiction? A lost love? Visits from the grandchildren? If I move away and visit, what will I think about? My ex-girlfriend? The books I wrote? The women in maid uniforms and nametags, shuffling toward the mailbox, too tired to smile?

. . .

The earth moves and my apartment shakes. Is this a dream? No. An earthquake? Maybe an 8.0. The chandeliers swing. The window shades rattle. The floorboards moan. In bed, I curl into the fetal position and close my eyes. Ten seconds later, when the apartment stops shaking, I open them. The closet-door mirrors come into focus. The alarm clock reads two-thirty-three a.m. On the horizon, a plume of dust and smoke rises where the Stardust stood for nearly 50 years.

. . .

Epitaphs for the Diplomat: "Home of the Stars ... and the Formerly Homeless," "There's No Place Like Home," and "It Wasn't Much, But It Beat the Streets."

Originally published on February 1, 2007, **"WHERE'S JESSIE?"** breathed some life into Foster's case. There were reported sightings of Jessie. A bounty hunter and another private investigator offered their services to her parents. And the case was covered by "The Montel Williams Show," the *National Enquirer*, "America's Most Wanted," E! and many other media outlets.

But Glendene Grant and Dwight Foster still don't know what happened to their daughter.

"Perhaps the most painful and disheartening thing about this case is that all the possible scenarios we discussed and envisioned are as valid and possible today as they were when we hired PI Mike Kirkman in April 2006," said Foster. "Nearly four years since my daughter's disappearance, and we're no closer to finding out what happened to her than we were back then."

In 2008, Grant and Foster waited for the autopsy results of a woman found in the Mojave Desert. It was thought Jessie may have been one of 13 bodies (including a fetus) discovered on the outskirts of Albuquerque, New Mexico, in early 2009. There's speculation she was the victim of a truck driver who preyed on Las Vegas prostitutes and dumped their bodies out of state.

A $50,000 reward. Desert searches. Jane Does. DNA samples. Months and months of waiting.

And in the end, like when they flew home from Vegas, Grant and Foster are left with more questions than answers.

"I really don't know what to think about where Jessie is anymore," said Grant, who's co-founded an organization (MATH) that raises awareness about human trafficking. "But I can tell you this: I *will* find my daughter—or die trying."

If you have any information about the disappearance of Jessie

Foster, call Crime Stoppers at 1-800-222-8477 or the North Las Vegas Police Department at 702-633-1773.

. . .

After reading **"HUNTING HUNTER,"** Thompson sent me a fax: "Excellent story! Let's work together again." So for *CityLife*'s June 5, 2002, issue, which marked the 30th anniversary of *Fear and Loathing in Las Vegas*, I interviewed him about the book, the city, drugs, politics, and other related (and unrelated) subjects. We kept in touch: We faxed occasionally; I added him to *CityLife*'s mailing list and tried to talk him into being a contributing editor; he'd call late at night with questions about Vegas.

But Thompson's strangest call came early one morning in June 2003. In town for the premiere of *Breakfast with Hunter*, a documentary about his life, he said he couldn't stand the Palms (where he was staying) and Las Vegas and was plotting his escape. Clearly, he had "the Fear."

"I can't take it anymore," said Thompson. "Can you get me a flight out of here, man?"

I told him I didn't have any "connections" at the airport, but I could give him a ride. He ignored my offer and started arguing with his wife Anita, using colorful, creative, and bruising language worthy of the author of *Fear and Loathing in Las Vegas*. Finally, he said he had to go and the phone went dead. We didn't talk again that weekend (and never discussed the call).

In September 2004, I asked Thompson to write the foreword to my first book, *Beneath the Neon: Life and Death in the Tunnels of Las Vegas* (Huntington Press, June 2007). He said he was too busy to write the foreword, but he'd write a blurb. Mail me the rough draft when it's done, he said.

I finished the draft on February 16, 2005. Four days later—before I had a chance to mail the manuscript—Thompson shot himself in the head at his home in Woody Creek, Colorado. His suicide note, titled "Football Season Is Over," read: "No More Games. No More Bombs. No More Walking. No More Fun. No More Swimming. 67.

That is 17 years past 50. 17 more than I needed or wanted. Boring. I am always bitchy. No Fun—for anybody. 67. You are getting Greedy. Act your old age. Relax—this won't hurt."

. . .

Thomas Paine's Church of God and Common Sense debuted in September 2005, as Larry LaPenta promised, but hosted only a handful of meetings and services. LaPenta caught pneumonia, was hospitalized, and died on January 2, 2006; his church died shortly thereafter. Its space is now occupied by the Las Vegas Church of the Harvest (tagline: "It's Time for Your Miracle!").

But LaPenta's name lives on in Larry's Villa, which is owned and operated by the Lawrence A. LaPenta Family Trust. Since his death, the Villa's become more upscale (a no-gang-colors dress code, new furniture, a VIP room). Nonetheless, it's still one of the cheapest, friendliest, and most casual strip clubs in Vegas.

. . .

I haven't stayed at the Blue Angel since that week in the spring of 2009, but I visit the motel occasionally. Only the faces have changed. I haven't seen Lisa since the cops escorted her off the property. Her roommate Dave got on that Greyhound to Colorado. Steve and his dog Dot have been playing musical motels: the Paradise, the Safari, the Ariza.

Even Mack, the German shepherd watchdog, ran away.

"No, I don't miss the Blue Angel," said Steve, who moved out in August '09. "It was just a stepping stone for me. You got to have a foundation, then you build up from there. If you can't build up, you fall into the gutter and you're like everybody else on the streets down here."

Steve still sees his doctors regularly and takes an assortment of meds. His knee-replacement surgery has been postponed, he said, as the VA tries to determine if surgery is necessary.

"Physically for me, it's one day at a time," said Steve. "I don't know what's going to happen tomorrow. I feel pretty good today, but tomorrow I could be dead. If so, I wouldn't complain. I feel like I've done everything I can do in life."

Sign designer Betty Willis is alive and kicking. As she guaranteed, the angel's still watching over the motel—but for how much longer? On May 19, 2010, the Las Vegas City Council approved a developer's plan to raze the motel and build 95,000 square feet of commercial space, including restaurants, shops, and a supermarket. The project, if financed, could move forward in the next two years. If it does, the 52-year-old guardian angel of east Fremont would most likely be incorporated into the project or preserved in the Neon Museum.

. . .

For a year and four months, Doaud Allison defied Nevada's recidivism rate and accomplished many of his goals. He became an apprentice with the Ironworkers Union. A steel company hired him as a welder. He got an apartment and his first car, a 2003 Pontiac Bonneville.

But in August 2006, Allison returned to prison on a parole violation (attempted possession of marijuana).

"Going to prison at age fifteen and being there for so long, I really didn't understand and know society," said Allison, now 33. "But being that I got out and was working, got my own apartment, a car, females, and everything, and it got taken away from me, I was missing things when I went back to prison. I was *really* missing my job. When I was held in the county jail, I could look out the window and watch ironworkers build things. That made me sick to my stomach."

Rereleased in April 2007, Allison went back to work at the steel company, but was laid off in the late summer of '08. A year later—on September 17—his first child, Mecca Fatima Allison, was born.

"I know what I've been through and I want to pave a better way for her," he said. "I don't want her to go through what I went through. I want her to be proud of her dad."

Allison gets work sporadically through the union and hopes to become a journeyman in a year or so. He also wants to earn a college degree.

"I'm just taking it one day at a time and hoping I can find a

Doaud Allison

niche," said Allison, who rents an apartment in northwest Vegas. "I'm cool with the iron work, but I don't want to bust my back all my life. I'm just keeping an eye on the economy, learning to adapt, and trying not to do anything illegal. That's what it's all about right now."

.   .   .

In 2006, the County Commission approved temporary measures to help tenants move when a trailer park closed: they were given nine months (instead of six); owners had to pay to move trailers up to 100 miles (instead of 50); and they were paid up to $1,500 (instead of nothing) for other relocation costs. And in 2007, the state legislature passed bills that made owners pay "fair market value" for trailers— plus (instead of minus) the cost of removal and disposal—and study how closing a park would affect tenants.

But the changes came late for most tenants.

After soaring for several years, land prices leveled off in 2007 and then plummeted. Developers and investment companies stopped buying trailer parks. In '07 and '08 combined, only four parks closed in Clark County. (Fourteen closed in '05.) There were no closings in '09.

"I think the manufactured-home industry is just like everything else today," said Marolyn Mann, executive director of Manufactured Home Community Owners. "We're treading water. Nobody's buying or selling. Everyone's just trying to stay afloat."

Many of the parks that closed are vacant; land prices are, once again, reasonable; and there's a need for affordable housing. (The unemployment rate in Las Vegas is 14%.) But a trailer-park renaissance seems unlikely. There are 1,700 vacant trailer spaces in the county, so demand is low, and other affordable-housing options: homes average $150,000, condos $75,000, and apartments $775 a month.

A trailer park hasn't opened in Clark County since 2000.

"I should be optimistic about the future of mobile-home parks in Las Vegas," said Mann. "There are a lot of seniors here and when you look at places like California and Arizona, you can't find better affordable housing than manufactured homes. But we have trouble with codes and zoning and other things like that. It just doesn't factor out on paper."

. . .

Josh and I talked about turning "**NOTES FROM VEGAS UNDERGROUND**" and "**BELLY OF THE BEAST**" into a book, but we decided against it. He was moving to San Francisco, we had different visions for the book, and having heard about married couples who got divorced while working on books together, we figured we'd end up killing each other.

So Josh passed the project off to me, with the understanding that if I got a book deal I'd give him a cut of the advance. I got a deal with Huntington Press, gave Josh his cut, and took a sabbatical from *CityLife* in the summer of 2004 to explore the underground flood channels on my own. The explorations continued through 2006 and formed the foundation of *Beneath the Neon*. The storm-drain stories provided background for the book, which has been reviewed or covered by more than 100 media outlets and is in its fourth printing.

In the spring of 2009, I founded Shine a Light, a community project that provides drug counseling, mental-health counseling, medical care, and other services to the hundreds of men and women living in the storm drains. The project—a collaboration with charity organization HELP of Southern Nevada—has housed more than 30 people.

For more info on Shine a Light, visit www.beneaththeneon.com.

. . .

The impact of the recession on the Las Vegas casino, construction, and real estate industries has been well-documented, but locals and tourists may not realize its reach: all the way to the central sewage plant.

In 2006, when I toured the plant, it was treating 100 million gallons of sewage a day—and rising. It now treats 90 million (despite the debut of the 67-acre, 7,200-unit CityCenter resort). Customer accounts have leveled off at 225,000. And some expansion and new projects have been postponed or canceled, said spokesman Marty Flynn.

"We're evaluating the impacts of the economic conditions on our decrease in flows," said Flynn. "We believe it's a cumulative effect of the specific impacts—a decrease in visitor volume and increase in vacant homes—but we're still analyzing the situation."

However, the plant hasn't laid off anyone, he said, and Deputy General Manager Doug Drury, Manager of Plant Operations Bill Shepherd, and Supervisor of Operations A. "Slick" Taylor still work there. Also, as frustrated drivers have no doubt noticed, the Water Reclamation District is keeping busy outside the plant: It's three years into a $108 million five-year plan to upgrade its pipelines.

One of the plant's challenges will be keeping pace with technology, said Flynn. As the ability to detect contaminants in sewage improves, it will create a need for new types of treatment.

But he's confident the plant will meet the challenge.

"There's a limited amount of water here," said Flynn. "It's precious. We have to take care of it."

. . .

In November 2008, a $17 million, 26,000-square-foot Metro Police substation opened at the corner of Sierra Vista and Swenson, just down the street from the Diplomat apartments. The substation is staffed by 110 officers, 30 detectives, and 20 supervisors and has helped fight crime in the neighborhood. However, in the spring of '09, two homeless men found a baby in a dumpster behind La Mesa apartments, a few hundred feet from the station. Twenty-one-month-old Shia Travis was stuffed in a pillowcase wearing only a Winnie-the-Pooh diaper. A few days later, police arrested 37-year-old William Marshall, who lived at the complex with Shia's mother. (Police found a matching pillowcase and Winnie-the-Pooh diapers in the apartment.)

Awaiting trial, Marshall is being held at the Clark County Detention Center. The mother has not been charged with a crime.

Farther west on Sierra Vista, at the 50-year-old Diplomat, things have been relatively quiet. Residents gossip about the widening of Paradise Road, which will consume the front parking lot and bring traffic closer, and the occupancy rate (not about the complex being sold, which seems unlikely in this economy). In May 2008, the occupancy rate was 95%. Now it's 70.

Evictions doubled during this same period.

"In March [2010] alone I've had five evictions," said co-manager Jan Hasner. "Normally I have one or two a month. It's getting serious. People are losing their jobs. They're skipping out in the middle of the night and going to live with family. One woman was crying this morning when she was evicted. I felt bad for her, but what can I do? I work with them till I can't work with them anymore."

All these people coming and going—my neighbor Don moved out in September '09, because he wasn't making enough money to pay the rent—but five years later, I'm still at the Diplomat. Still staring at the Strip ... and dreaming.

MATTHEW O'BRIEN | JUNE 11, 2010

ABOUT THE AUTHOR

Matthew O'Brien is an author and journalist who's lived in Las Vegas since 1997.

His first book, *Beneath the Neon: Life and Death in the Tunnels of Las Vegas*, chronicles his adventures in the city's underground flood channels, which he explored for more than four years with a flashlight, tape recorder, and expandable baton for protection.

My Week at the Blue Angel: And Other Stories from the Storm Drains, Strip Clubs, and Trailer Parks of Las Vegas is his second book.

He's the founder of Shine a Light, a community project that provides housing, drug counseling, and other services to the people living in the drains.

For more info on Matt and his books, visit www.beneaththeneon.com.

ABOUT THE PHOTOGRAPHER

Bill Hughes is an award-winning photojournalist who moved from Dallas to Las Vegas in 1992 and worked for the alternative weekly newspaper *CityLife* until 2009.

His work has also appeared in publications including the *L.A. Times* and newspapers in the Village Voice media chain.